Fodor's

salt lake city AND THE
wasatch range

Excerpted from Fodor's *Rockies*

fodor's travel publications
new york · toronto · london · sydney · auckland
www.fodors.com

contents

ON THE ROAD WITH FODOR'S

THE MORE YOU KNOW BEFORE YOU GO, the better your trip will be. Salt Lake City's most fascinating small museum (or the Wasatch Front's most superlative ski slope) could be just around the corner from your hotel, but if you don't know it's there, it might as well be on the other side of the globe. That's where this book comes in. It's a great step toward making sure your next trip lives up to your expectations. As you plan, check out the Web as well. Guidebooks have been helping smart travelers find the special places for years; the Web is one more tool. Whatever reference you consult, be savvy about what you read, and always consider the source. Images and language can be massaged to make places appear better than they are. And one traveler's quaint is another's grimy.

Here at Fodor's, and at our on-line arm, Fodors.com, our focus is on providing you with information that's not only useful but accurate and on target. Every day Fodor's editors put enormous effort into getting things right, beginning with the search for the right contributors—people who have objective judgment, broad travel experience, and the writing ability to put their insights into words. There's no substitute for advice from a like-minded friend who has just come back from where you're going, but our writers, having seen all corners of Salt Lake City and the Wasatch Front, are the next best thing. They're the kind of people you'd poll for tips yourself if you knew them.

Kate Boyes has lived in Utah since 1982 and spends her free time hiking, biking, skiing, whitewater rafting, and gathering ideas for screenplays. Her commentaries on life in the Rockies air regularly on Utah Public Radio, and her essays on art, nature, and outdoor recreation have appeared in numerous magazines and anthologies, including *Great & Peculiar Beauty* and *American Nature Writing*. Her home base is Smithfield, Utah.

Gayen and Tom Wharton are based in Salt Lake City, where Tom is a reporter for *The Salt Lake Tribune* and Gayen is a freelance writer. They have co-authored several books about their home state, including *Compass American Guide to Utah*, *Utah Camping*, *Utah—A Family Travel Guide*, and *It Happened in Utah*. Gayen recently published *Dinosaurs of Utah* and *Dino Destinations* with Pat Bagley.

Don't Forget to Write

Keeping a travel guide fresh and up-to-date is a big job. So we love your feedback—positive and negative—and follow up on all suggestions. Contact the Salt Lake City editor at editors@fodors.com or c/o Fodor's, 280 Park Avenue, New York, New York 10017. And have a wonderful trip!

Karen Cure

Editorial Director

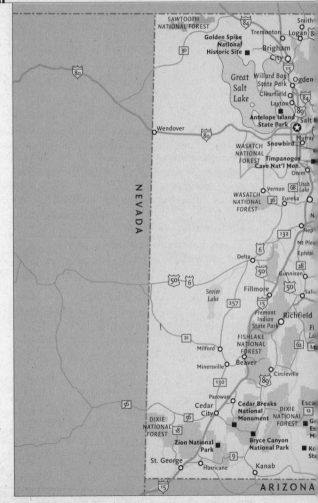

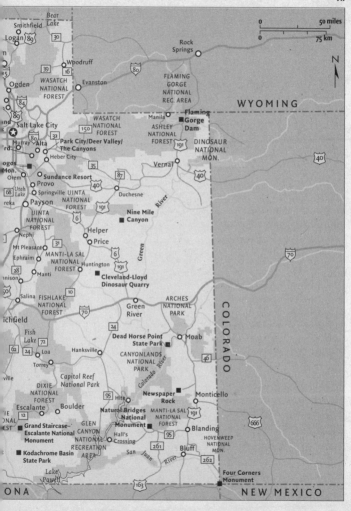

salt lake city AND THE
wasatch range

It's impossible to fully appreciate Utah's magnificent natural and cultural heritage without understanding the spirit of the people who transformed what many regarded as a wasteland into a thriving state. This is truly a land of the pioneers.

In This Chapter

By Tom and Gayen Wharton

introducing salt lake city and the wasatch

IN THE MID-19TH CENTURY, NEWCOMERS FROM ACROSS THE PLAINS
brought Utah a distinctive, energetic spirit that the Native
Americans, the Catholic explorers and priests, and the independent
mountain men who preceded them might have respected. Brigham
Young arrived on July 24, 1847, with 143 men, 3 women, 2 children,
70 wagons, 1 boat, 1 cannon, 93 horses, 52 mules, 66 oxen, and
19 cows. He went on to build Salt Lake City from almost nothing,
laying it out in wide, square, well-organized blocks. He sent
followers out to remote corners of the unsettled West, and their
faith and their willingness to work hard gave them the courage
to face the unknown.

These pioneers sought freedom to worship in their own way,
and dreamed of turning these lands into a modern-day Zion
through hard work and community effort. The miners, soldiers,
railroad workers, and others who came later may not have held
the same religious beliefs, but they were certainly caught up in
the pioneering spirit. All who came here learned how to make a
living from the land.

Today, on the east bench of Salt Lake City, a weathered statue
gazes silently at the valley below. The blue waters of the Great
Salt Lake and the mighty peaks of the Wasatch Front are still
visible, as they were when Young first looked out from this spot
and ended his perilous 1,500-mile journey by declaring, "This is

the place." Could even a visionary such as Young have imagined what Salt Lake City—or all Utah—would become?

Through the ages, all those who have made Utah their home have had the courageous spirit of true pioneers. The state brings out a conservative, independent streak in people: its official motto is "Industry"; its official symbol is the beehive. Utahns take their work seriously.

Witness the Greek musician Maurice Abravanel, who came to the state with the desire to build a world-renowned symphony orchestra and who did not retire until his dream became reality. Or consider the team of researchers and doctors who created the first artificial heart and successfully implanted it in a living human being. And remember people like Utah Jazz owner Larry Miller, who spent much of his own money to open the glittering Delta Center in the early 1990s, revitalizing the western part of Salt Lake City.

You can see the work ethic and the pioneering spirit everywhere. Walk down the clean streets of Salt Lake, where dozens of new buildings have arisen and where business executives and government leaders plot the state's course for the 21st century. Listen to a symphony, or attend a play, an opera, or ballet. Then escape to the wild lands of the Wasatch Front and beyond. As you hike along a forest trail, bounce up and down in a jeep on a ride through a canyon, or stand at the site where the transcontinental railroad was completed in 1869, you, too, may catch the spirit.

PORTRAITS

LDS LEGACIES

The pioneers of the Church of Jesus Christ of Latter-Day Saints—the Mormons—dramatically changed Utah's landscape. Unlike the original Native American and mountain man inhabitants,

Utah Has the Zs

Conventionally, repeats of the letter z suggest snoring or sound sleep, not athleticism. Things are different in Utah, however, where many of the sports teams' names end with a double z. The trend started in 1979 when the National Basketball Association's (NBA's) New Orleans Jazz moved to the state. Few thought the team would retain the name. After all, the Beehive State isn't a hotbed of jazz music. Indeed, the folks in New Orleans scoffed at the relationship as well as the idea of the team keeping its Mardi Gras–color uniforms.

But after considering new names such as the Seagulls, the Pioneers, or the Saints (another that would have no doubt upset New Orleans fans), the owners retained the Jazz moniker. Utah's only major-league professional team turned into one of the NBA's top franchises a few years later, making the name a familiar one around the country. What's more, it started a trend.

The Jazz's counterpart in the Women's NBA became known as the Utah Starzz. The state's venerable professional hockey franchise, first known as the Salt Lake Golden Eagles, was renamed the Utah Grizzlies, or Grizz for short. The Utah Blitzz is a men's professional soccer team, and the Utah Freezz play in the World Indoor Soccer League. Although one team has reversed the trend—the minor-league baseball team formerly known as the Buzz is now called the Stingers—expect other franchises and teams to eye Utah's burgeoning market and, perhaps, give it still more z's.

the Mormons set out to make the dry Salt Lake Valley look more like their previous homes back east. They dammed streams and rivers to irrigate crops. They constructed mills to do everything from grind wheat to mill lumber to make buttons. Towns and cities sprouted at the mouth of every canyon. Additional settlements grew with the flood of converts from England and Scandinavia.

Today the valleys where trees once grew only along stream banks are filled with an urban forest, and the state's top attraction is Temple Square, headquarters of the Mormon Church. Here you can listen to the famous Mormon Tabernacle Choir, research your roots at the genealogical library—one of the most complete facilities of its kind in the world—or stroll through the attractive Temple Grounds. Clean streets and plenty of urban landscaping are traditions passed down from the early pioneers.

Although the percentage of Mormons in the state has dropped and is lowest in Salt Lake City, don't be surprised if one of the first questions you're asked is whether you're Mormon. If you're not, try to be open-minded and understanding. Religion is a big topic of discussion here, and the Church still plays a key role in both politics and business. Laws governing liquor, entertainment, sex education, and pornography reflect the majority's religious values.

Recruiting volunteers with foreign-language skills for work during the Olympics wasn't difficult for organizers thanks to one Mormon legacy—an extensive worldwide missionary program. Those sent to foreign lands must learn the language of the host country, where they will live for two years. On returning home they often jump at the chance to use their second tongue. In fact, the U.S. Army relies on the Utah National Guard's linguistic unit for many of its translation needs.

While the missionaries head out, many converts head in, lending the region an international flavor. Recent census figures

Mormon Munchies

The Mormon religion has helped to shape the state's cuisine as well as its culture. The church advises followers to refrain from drinking beverages containing alcohol or caffeine. Some people theorize that this has led to the development of a collective sweet tooth. Sweet red punch is perhaps the state's most popular beverage, ice cream is consumed in great quantities (though the weight-conscious have switched to frozen yogurt), and shops that serve fresh pastries are all the rage.

Green Jell-O gelatin—topped with miniature marshmallows and mixed with grated carrots or cottage cheese and pineapple—appears at every Mormon social function. In 2001, when Salt Lake City lost its title as the number-one consumer of Jell-O to Des Moines, Iowa, the state legislature got into the act. During a visit by Jell-O Company spokesman and comedian Bill Cosby, lawmakers declared the wiggly stuff as Utah's official state snack. The tide turned and for the time being, more of the stuff is consumed per capita than in any other state.

At family functions such as potluck dinners, weddings, and funerals you'll often see a dish that's dubbed "funeral potatoes." It's made from potatoes, cheddar cheese, canned soup, and sour cream—all baked and covered with buttered bread crumbs. One favorite that's readily available at restaurants is fry sauce. The originator of a local hamburger chain, Arctic Circle, invented this combination of ketchup, mayonnaise, and spices. It caught on, and most locals demand the sauce for their french fries at all burger joints.

show that a large number of Latin American and Polynesian converts have arrived. In recent years. A robust economy and the presence of active philanthropic institutions have brought additional immigrants from the Balkans, the Middle East, Tibet, the former Soviet Union, Southeast Asia, and Africa. Add to this the Irish, Italian, Greek, Chinese, Japanese, and Mexican workers who once migrated here to mine, farm, or work on railroads and you have quite a cultural mix.

Polygamy was once widely practiced among the Mormons. This was, and still is, a controversial issue. Hundreds of fundamentalist Mormons continue the practice, and occasionally a story comes to light about its negative aspects, such as large families taking part in welfare fraud or older men arranging marriages with girls as young as 13. Although polygamy is not condoned, it's hard for anyone with roots in the state to question the practice too vigorously—this might mean questioning their ancestors' faith and actions.

A LAND FOR ALL TIMES

There's more than intuition behind the claim that Alta, Snowbird, Park City, and other Utah resorts have the best snow in the world. There's science behind it, too. The secret to Utah's famous powder is in the structure of the snow crystals. Atmospheric conditions over this part of the western United States are usually cold and relatively dry. Light snowflakes called dendrites are formed under these conditions and fall to earth in layers with lots of air between them. Skiing through such light powder feels like floating through clouds. This is why many feel that Utah has the best snow on the planet. Although the area's downhill skiing receives most of the attention, snowmobiling, cross-country skiing, and snowshoeing are other popular powder-snow pursuits.

The snow stops falling in April or May, and a month later the temperatures are in the '80s. (Locals joke that if don't like the weather in the spring, wait a minute and it will change.) Spring may be the shortest season, but it's one of the most interesting. You can ski in the morning, play 18 holes of golf in the afternoon, and take a sunset dinner cruise on the Great Salt Lake. Sun worshippers flock to huge city parks to get started on their tans. Hikers and horseback riders enjoy trips to Dimple Dell Park on the south end of Salt Lake Valley, where sego lilies, the state flower, bloom in June.

In summer, water-sports enthusiasts of all stripes flock to the region. Many of the parks in the Wasatch Front are on reservoirs, and alpine lakes, rivers, and streams teem with trout. The Wasatch Mountains also draw hikers seeking respite from the heat of the valley, where temperatures hit 90°F or higher (the mercury rises to more than 100°F nearly every July). Summer in Salt Lake City means a float on the Great Salt Lake. At the beach in Antelope Island State Park, north of town, you can simply sit down in the water and bob to the surface like a rubber duck. The salinity level fluctuates from 6% to 27% but is always greater than that of the ocean, and this makes the water extremely buoyant.

Fall's colors rival those of New England. On a walk through a forest or drive along a scenic route, you'll see the yellows, reds, oranges, and golds of aspens, maples, oaks, and other trees against the deep green of pine, fir, and spruce. This is a wonderful time for a picnic in City Creek Canyon, a short walk from downtown Salt Lake, or one of five other canyons east of town. Fall drives to Monte Cristo east of Ogden, along the Alpine Loop east of Provo, or up Logan Canyon are autumn traditions.

Regardless of the season, you can find arts and cultural activities at every turn. In Salt Lake, the warmer months see concert series, farmers' markets, and street fairs. The city is one of the few between the Mississippi and California that can boast of having a distinguished symphony orchestra, a ballet company, and numerous modern dance, opera, and acting troupes. Most

Your checklist for a perfect journey

WAY AHEAD
- Devise a trip budget.
- Write down the five things you want most from this trip. Keep this list handy before and during your trip.
- Make plane or train reservations. Book lodging and rental cars.
- Arrange for pet care.
- Check your passport. Apply for a new one if necessary.
- Photocopy important documents and store in a safe place.

A MONTH BEFORE
- Make restaurant reservations and buy theater and concert tickets. Visit fodors.com for links to local events.
- Familiarize yourself with the local language or lingo.

TWO WEEKS BEFORE
- Replenish your supply of medications.
- Create your itinerary.
- Enjoy a book or movie set in your destination to get you in the mood.
- Develop a packing list. Shop for missing essentials. Repair and launder or dry-clean your clothes.

A WEEK BEFORE
- Stop newspaper deliveries. Pay bills.
- Acquire traveler's checks.
- Stock up on film.
- Label your luggage.
- Finalize your packing list— take less than you think you need.
- Create a toiletries kit filled with travel-size essentials.
- Get lots of sleep. Don't get sick before your trip.

A DAY BEFORE
- Drink plenty of water.
- Check your travel documents.
- Get packing!

DURING YOUR TRIP
- Keep a journal/scrapbook.
- Spend time with locals.
- Take time to explore. Don't plan too much.

Broadway touring companies include Salt Lake on their schedules. Major recording artists of all types make it to one of the big arenas along the Wasatch Front; some of these venues are also home to major- or minor-league sports teams. The Sundance Film Festival, produced by actor Robert Redford, attracts movie stars and independent filmmakers from all over and seems to get bigger every January.

There are an increasing number of nightclubs featuring everything from hard rock music to folk. An area west of Salt Lake City's main downtown has many such clubs. Ogden and Park City offer even more nightlife possibilities. A variety of bars, brew pubs, and private clubs dot Ogden's historic 25th Street and Park City's Main Street.

Although winter's powder snows are famous, Salt Lake City and the Wasatch Front are year-round destinations. Spring meadows offer dramatic wildflower displays; summer lakes are cool, blue, and inviting; and fall trees light up the mountains with their vivid colors.

In This Chapter

By Tom and Gayen Wharton

perfect days

ARE YOU PERPLEXED ABOUT WHICH SKI RESORT IS BEST? Or are you wondering about what to do in summer? Below are some suggestions for flawless days, regardless of when you travel.

A PERFECT WINTER DAY

When there's fresh snow in the Wasatch, all seems right with the world. Whether or not you ski, be sure to spend time playing in the snow.

Drive to Park City and spend most of the day skiing or snowboarding the slopes of Park City Mountain Resort or The Canyons; for a skiing-only spot, Deer Valley is the place. If you don't ski, head for the Utah Winter Sports Park to catch a U.S. Bobsled Team practice. Or take a ride yourself while team members steer.

Later in the day, hop the Park City shuttle down to Main Street. Make dinner reservations (the earlier the better) at Grappa if you like Italian, Chimayo if you crave Mexican, or 350 Main if you hanker for seafood. Spend the rest of the day wandering along this slice of the Old West and shopping in its small, exclusive stores.

A PERFECT SPRING DAY

When the pioneers first arrived in 1847, Brigham Young claimed he would make the desert blossom like a rose. His descendents have decked Salt Lake City with many a flower garden—making it a great place to explore when the trees start to bud.

In the morning, board a horse-drawn carriage on South Temple for a ride around Temple Square and its environs. Afterward, tour the Museum of Church History and/or the Beehive House. Pick up a copy of the *Salt Lake Tribune, The Deseret News,* or *City Weekly* before heading to the restaurant atop the Joseph Smith Memorial Building for lunch (note that the building is closed on Sunday).

During your meal, study the paper to see what's happening in the evening. Make arrangements to see a show or a sporting event, and make dinner reservations at the Metropolitan restaurant. Afterward, walk along broad, tree-lined Main Street. South of Temple Square are two malls, the Crossroads Plaza and ZCMI Center. They're across the street from one another and within sight of the Temple. Spend the afternoon shopping here, or take a walk up State Street to the capitol.

A PERFECT SUMMER DAY

The beaches of the Great Salt Lake are unlike any in the world. Yes, there are gulls squawking overhead, and there's blue water as far as you can see. But the water is much saltier than the ocean and its deepest point is around 35 feet. You can readily spend a summer's day bobbing about in it.

In the morning, make reservations for a Salt Island Adventures dinner cruise, pack a picnic lunch, and drive to Antelope Island State Park, about 30 minutes north of Salt Lake City. After a stop at the visitor center, wander along the Buffalo Point Trail, which may provide you glimpses of buffalo, coyotes, or pronghorn antelope. You're almost certain to hear meadowlarks singing in the sagebrush.

Have lunch in one of the sheltered picnic areas along the shore. Afterward, experience the sensation of weightlessness with a float in the lake. (Don't put your head under water, though, as the salt will really sting your eyes). Nap for a while on the pellet-like oolitic sand. Return to Salt Lake and take Exit 104 off I-80 to the South Shore State Park and the South Shore Marina.

During your dinner cruise aboard Salt Island Adventures' 65-ft boat, you can watch the sun set over the islands to the west and catch the alpenglow on the Wasatch Mountains to the east while you feast on prime rib or chicken.

A PERFECT FALL DAY

Few places in the world are as beautiful as the Wasatch Mountains in September and October. Seize the day to luxuriate in the bright colors and crisp temperatures. Pack a picnic lunch, make dinner reservations at the Tree Room restaurant, and head out on the Alpine Loop Scenic Byway, Route 92, from American Fork Canyon to Provo Canyon.

There are several hiking options off this byway. If you're ambitious, head to Timpanogos Cave National Monument in American Fork Canyon and follow the trail to Timpanogos Cave or hike from the Aspen Grove trailhead to the first waterfall on 11,788-ft Mt. Timpanogos. If you have less stamina, stroll along the boardwalk at Cascade Springs, a short drive off the Alpine Loop, or take a trip on the 100-year-old, steam-powered Heber Valley Historic Railroad.

The train runs twice a day and departs from 450 South 600 West Street in Heber City (be sure to make reservations). It snakes along the shore of Deer Creek Reservoir and parallels the Provo River as it plunges down narrow Provo Canyon. The train's snack car sells everything from barbecue sandwiches to ice cream.

Smart Sightseeings

Savvy travelers and others who take their sightseeing seriously have skills worth knowing about.

DON'T PLAN YOUR VISIT IN YOUR HOTEL ROOM Don't wait until you pull into town to decide how to spend your days. It's inevitable that there will be much more to see and do than you'll have time for: choose sights in advance.

ORGANIZE YOUR TOURING Note the places that most interest you on a map, and visit places that are near each other during the same morning or afternoon.

START THE DAY WELL EQUIPPED Leave your hotel in the morning with everything you need for the day—maps, medicines, extra film, your guidebook, rain gear, and another layer of clothing in case the weather turns cooler.

TOUR MUSEUMS EARLY If you're there when the doors open you'll have an intimate experience of the collection.

EASY DOES IT See museums in the mornings, when you're fresh, and visit sit-down attractions later on. Take breaks before you need them.

STRIKE UP A CONVERSATION Only curmudgeons don't respond to a smile and a polite request for information. Most people appreciate your interest in their home town. And your conversations may end up being your most vivid memories.

GET LOST When you do, you never know what you'll find—but you can count on it being memorable. Use your guidebook to help you get back on track. Build wandering-around time into every day.

QUIT BEFORE YOU'RE TIRED There's no point in seeing that one extra sight if you're too exhausted to enjoy it.

TAKE YOUR MOTHER'S ADVICE Go to the bathroom when you have the chance. You never know what lies ahead.

In the evening, visit actor Robert Redford's Sundance Resort. Redford came to Utah to film a movie about mountain man Jeremiah Johnson. He fell in love with Mt. Timpanogos, which guards Sundance, and bought the resort. The Continental cuisine and the collection of Native American and Western memorabilia at the resort's Tree Room restaurant make for a memorable meal.

Balance—between urban polish and rugged wilderness, between progress and tradition—is key in this city. Its streets may be modern, but they're also tidy and tree-lined. Its high-rises may tower and shine, but their size is dwarfed by the Wasatch Mountains to the east, and their sparkle is outshone by the Great Salt Lake to the northwest.

In This Chapter

Updated by Kate Boyes

salt lake city

SALT LAKE HAS COME OF AGE. In the last decade, the population has climbed to more than 800,000, a dynamic skyline has sprouted, the rings of suburbia have widened, and fashionable retail enclaves have arisen. Restaurants now serve up a world of tastes, the nightlife is worthy of discussion, and the community takes great pride in its NBA team, the Utah Jazz, as well its role as host of the 2002 Olympic Winter Games. Although it's the headquarters of the Church of Jesus Christ of Latter-Day Saints—the Mormons—people of all spiritual bents and ethnicities travel here; quite a few have chosen to call it home. This has lent a cultural diversity that many find surprising.

While emerging as a major Rocky Mountain hub, however, Salt Lake has maintained the charm of a much smaller town. Landmark 19th-century buildings have been preserved, and this in turn has kept the community's historic soul intact. The city's wide streets are clean, and its residents value mass transit, the arts, and parks so much that they've voted for two sales-tax increases in recent years to provide for such urban amenities. And, as one commuter marveled, it's impossible to get much reading done on the train because fellow passengers keep striking up conversations. Strangers, it seems, quickly become friends in this town.

HERE AND THERE

Like many other Utah municipalities, Salt Lake is based on a grid plan devised by Brigham Young in the 19th century. Most street names have a numerical and a directional designation describing their location in relation to one of two axes. Streets with "East" or "West" in their names are east or west of (and parallel to) Main Street, which runs north–south, while "North" and "South" streets run parallel to South Temple Street. The numbers tell how far the streets are from these axes. For example, 200 East Street is two blocks east of Main Street.

Addresses typically include two numerical references and two directional references; 320 East 200 South Street, for instance, is in the east 300 block of 200 South Street. Three of Salt Lake's most prominent streets are named after the Mormon Temple: North Temple, South Temple, and West Temple, indicating that the streets border Temple Square on the north, south, and west. Main Street runs along the square's east side.

Numbers in the text and in the margins correspond to points of interest on the Salt Lake City and Salt Lake City Environs maps.

DOWNTOWN SALT LAKE

Although businesses and homes stretch in all directions, downtown's core is a compact, four-block-by-four-block area that includes several buildings central to Mormonism, two large malls, historic buildings, and entertainment venues.

A Good Walk

TEMPLE SQUARE ① is a good place to begin a walking tour of the city. Across West Temple Street are two Mormon-owned and -operated institutions: the **MUSEUM OF CHURCH HISTORY AND ART** ② and the **FAMILY HISTORY LIBRARY** ③. East of Temple Square across Main Street is the **JOSEPH SMITH MEMORIAL BUILDING** ④. Dominating that block is the **LDS CHURCH OFFICE BUILDING** ⑤. Farther east, just across State

Living Traditions

Each year on the third weekend in May, Salt Lake City celebrates its cultural diversity with the Living Traditions Festival. The Utah Humanities Council started the festival to spotlight traditional folk arts, to enable ethnic minorities to express pride in their heritages, and to educate the public about the richness of the city's many cultures.

In the heart of the city, at Washington Square, 20-odd food vendors, each representing a nonprofit community group, prepare different national specialties. Money raised goes toward funding each group's activities throughout the year. On the four stages set up around the square, musicians and dancers from more than 45 countries perform. Past festivals have showcased performing arts from Brazil, Tahiti, Bosnia, Japan, and Norway. Artisans conduct demonstrations under tents and answer questions about their work on everything from Hopi kachina dolls and Tibetan rugs to Tongan mats and Japanese origami. One tent is set up as a crafts market.

Living Traditions is just one of Salt Lake's many annual ethnic festivals. The second week of September sees a Greek Festival, with food, dancing, and music. The suburb of Murray hosts a Scottish Festival during the second week of June. The St. Patrick's Day Parade, held the Saturday closest to March 17, turns the streets green with colorful floats, bands, and good humor, and there are numerous Cinco de Mayo festivals in the area.

—By Tom and Gayen Wharton

Street, are **BRIGHAM YOUNG HISTORIC PARK AND CITY CREEK PARK** ⑥. Two blocks south on State Street is the **BEEHIVE HOUSE** ⑦, once Brigham Young's official residence. If you take a 15-minute detour walk east along South Temple Street, you'll pass many fine buildings before reaching **KEARNS MANSION** ⑧, now the Utah governor's residence. Half a block south of the Beehive House is **HANSEN PLANETARIUM** ⑨. A block and a half farther south, on the west side of State Street at 200 South Street, is the **GALLIVAN CENTER** ⑩, an outdoor gathering place with year-round activities. Continue south on State Street to the middle of the 300 South block and turn right to see the **EXCHANGE PLACE HISTORIC DISTRICT** ⑪. Half a block south on State Street you can picnic or take a rest on the beautiful grounds of the **CITY AND COUNTY BUILDING** ⑫.

Salt Lake City's two enormous train stations attest to the fierce competition between railroads for dominance in the region. The **RIO GRANDE DEPOT** ⑬ is at the west end of 300 South Street. From here, head up 400 West Street for three blocks to the **UNION PACIFIC RAILROAD DEPOT** ⑭. Heading back toward Temple Square, you'll see the modern **DELTA CENTER** ⑮, at 300 West and South Temple Street, and the **SALT PALACE** ⑯ just south of South Temple Street on West Temple Street. These are the current and former homes, respectively, of the Utah Jazz. Each offers visitor information and sells good-quality Utah souvenirs.

TIMING

Allot half a day to enjoy downtown, not because it's a big area (it's not) but because it's historic, interesting, and pretty in any season.

What to See

❼ **BEEHIVE HOUSE.** Brigham Young's home, a national historic landmark, was constructed in 1854 and is topped with a replica of a beehive, symbolizing industry. Inside are many original furnishings, and a tour of the interior will give you a fascinating glimpse of upper-class, 19th-century, polygamous life. Young built the Lion House next door for some of his wives and children; it's now a social center and restaurant. 67 E. South Temple St., tel. 801/240–2672. Free. Mon.–Sat. 9:30–4:30, Sun. 10–1.

❻ BRIGHAM YOUNG HISTORIC PARK AND CITY CREEK PARK. These tiny twin parks divided by Second Avenue are a pretty diversion from the cityscape. Paths are inlaid with the footprints and names of native animals and birds, and a stone-lined stream drives a lazy mill wheel. East side of State St. at North Temple St.

OFF THE BEATEN PATH **CHILDREN'S MUSEUM OF UTAH** – The museum's goal is to "create the love of learning through hands-on experience," and that's exactly what it does. Children can pilot a jetliner, draw with computers, dig for mammoth bones, or lose themselves in the many other interactive exhibits. Admission is free on Friday after 5 PM. 840 N. 300 West St., tel. 801/328–3383, www.childmuseum.org. $3.75. Mon.–Thurs. and Sat. 10–6, Fri. 10–8.

⓬ CITY AND COUNTY BUILDING. The seat of city government is on Washington Square, at the spot where the original Mormon settlers circled their wagons on their first night in the Salt Lake Valley. Said to be modeled after London's City Hall, the structure has details common to the Romanesque Revival style. Construction began in 1892 and continued for two years. After Utah achieved statehood in 1896, the building served as the capitol for 19 years until the current capitol could be built. Hundreds of trees, including species from around the world, and many winding paths and seating areas make the grounds a cool downtown oasis. State St. between 400 and 500 South Sts.

⓯ DELTA CENTER. From the outside, this structure, built in the early 1990s, resembles an enormous block of ice. But from the inside the city and mountain views are stunning. Most people look inward, though, as the Delta Center arena seats 20,000 and is

salt lake city

N

TO THE
CHILDREN'S
MUSEUM OF
UTAH

← TO GREAT SALT LAKE
North Temple

← TO AIRPORT

8th Ave.
7th Ave.
6th Ave.
5th Ave.
4th Ave.
3rd Ave.
2nd Ave.
South Temple
100 South

TO UNIVERSITY →
OF UTAH
200 South

Victory Rd.
Canyon Rd.
A St.
B St.
C St.

Visitor
Information
Center

400 West
300 West
200 West
West Temple
Main St.
State St.
200 East
300 East

300 South

400 South

500 South

600 South

Lion
House

the home court for the NBA Utah Jazz and the WNBA Utah Starzz. Concerts, rodeos, ice shows, and other events are also held here. An information desk and a gift shop—with the city's best assortment of Utah Jazz paraphernalia—are open daily. *300 W. South Temple St., tel. 801/325–7328.*

⑪ **EXCHANGE PLACE HISTORIC DISTRICT.** With columns, carved figures, and both angles and curves, the massive stone buildings in Exchange Place are reminiscent of New York City's Wall Street historic district. Salt Lake's first skyscrapers—the Boston and Newhouse buildings—are here. Although today's high-rises make them seem small, they're an important part of what was, in the early 1900s, one of the West's leading commercial hubs. Today the quiet street has restaurants, shops, and an art gallery. *Between State and Main Sts. at 350 South St. Access is from State St. only.*

③ **FAMILY HISTORY LIBRARY.** Genealogy is important to Mormons because they believe in baptizing people, even after death. This library houses the world's largest collection of genealogical data. Mormons and non-Mormons alike come here to do research. *35 N. West Temple St., tel. 801/240–2331 or 800/537–9703, www.familysearch.org. Free. Mon. 7:30–5, Tues.–Sat. 7:30–10.*

⑩ **GALLIVAN CENTER.** This outdoor plaza hosts lunchtime and evening concerts, farmers' markets, and unique arts and crafts activities for all ages. It also has an ice rink and a giant outdoor chessboard. *36 E. 200 South St., tel. 801/532–0459. Free. Daily 7 AM– 10 PM.*

⑨ **HANSEN PLANETARIUM.** The domed theater and the moon-rock displays are just some of the stargazing delights here. Special events include laser shows set to music and live stage performances. There's also a great book and gift shop. *15 S. State St., tel. 801/538–2104, www.hansenplanetarium.org. Free; shows $2.50– $7.50. Mon.–Thurs. 9 AM–10 PM, Fri. and Sat. 9:30 AM–midnight, Sun. 11:30–6.*

④ JOSEPH SMITH MEMORIAL BUILDING. Once the Hotel Utah, this building on the National Historic Register is now owned and operated by the Mormon Church. You can use a computer program to learn how to do genealogical research, or watch an hour-long film on early Mormon history and the emigration of Mormons to the Salt Lake Valley in the mid-19th century. The center also has two restaurants and an elegantly restored lobby. *South Temple and Main Sts., tel. 801/240–1266 or 800/537–9703. Free. Mon.–Sat. 9–9.*

⑧ KEARNS MANSION. Built by silver-mining tycoon Thomas Kearns in 1902, this limestone structure reminiscent of a French château— all turrets and balconies—is now the official residence of Utah's governor. In its early days the mansion was visited by President Theodore Roosevelt and other dignitaries from around the world. A devastating fire in 1993 damaged much of the interior. Restoration took three years and included faithful re-creation of the colors and patterns used in the original decor and reconstruction of the golden dome that illuminates the central stairwell. *603 E. South Temple St., tel. 801/538–1005. Free. Tours Apr.– Nov., Tues. and Thurs. 2–4.*

⑤ LDS CHURCH OFFICE BUILDING. Standing 28 stories high, this is one of Salt Lake's tallest structures. Tours include a stop at the 26th-floor observation deck and, in spring through fall, visits to the lovely plaza gardens. Indicative of the breadth of the church's business dealings and the volume of mail it receives, this building has its own zip code. *50 E. North Temple St., tel. 801/240–2190. Free. June–Aug., Mon.–Sat. 9–4:30; Sept.–May, weekdays 9–4:30.*

② MUSEUM OF CHURCH HISTORY AND ART. The museum houses a variety of artifacts and works of art relating to the history and doctrine of the Mormon faith, including personal belongings of church leaders Joseph Smith, Brigham Young, and others. There are also samples of Mormon coins and scrip used as standard currency in Utah during the 1800s, and beautiful examples of quilting, embroidery, and other handwork. Upstairs galleries exhibit religious and secular works by Mormon artists from all over the world. 45 N. West Temple St., tel. 801/240–3310. Free. Weekdays 9–9, weekends 10–7.

⑬ RIO GRANDE DEPOT. This 1910 depot was built to compete with the showy Union Pacific Railroad Depot three blocks north. It houses the **Utah State Historical Society Museum,** which has rotating exhibits on the history of Utah and the West. An eclectic gift shop sells everything from scholarly works to reproductions of Victorian paper dolls and of sepia-tone photographs from the society's extensive collection. 300 S. Rio Grande St., tel. 801/533–3500. Free. Weekdays 8–5, Sat. 10–3.

⑯ SALT PALACE. The former home of the Utah Jazz has received a massive face-lift and expansion, and it is now an elegant convention center that includes a ballroom. Frequently the site of large consumer shows, community events, and factory-outlet sales, it also has a visitor information desk and a shop that sells Utah-theme books and gifts of better than average quality. 100 S. West Temple St., tel. 801/534–4777, www.saltpalace.com.

❶ TEMPLE SQUARE. Brigham Young chose this spot for a temple upon arriving in the Salt Lake Valley, but work on the building didn't begin for another six years. Built of blocks of granite hauled by oxen and train from Little Cottonwood Canyon, the Mormon Temple took 40 years to the day to complete. Its walls are 16 ft thick at the base. Perched 210 ft above ground level is a gilt statue of the trumpeting angel Moroni. Off-limits to all but faithful Mormons, the temple is used for marriages, baptisms, and other religious functions. Non-Mormons can learn more about the activities within at the North and South visitor centers. Dioramas, photos, a baptismal font, and other displays offer considerable insight into the Mormon religion.

Other buildings of interest at Temple Square include the Assembly Hall, completed in 1882 with leftover granite from the temple, and the Tabernacle, home of the world-renowned Mormon Tabernacle Choir. This unusual domed structure was built in the 1860s as a meeting place. Free of interior supports, the 8,000-seat building is known for its exquisite acoustics.

Impressive as the architectural trappings of Temple Square are, the 10-acre grounds are also most enjoyable. Don't be surprised if a member of the Church politely asks if you have any interest in learning more about Mormonism. *50 W. North Temple St., tel. 801/240–2534. Free. Daily 9–9.*

⑭ UNION PACIFIC RAILROAD DEPOT. This now-vacant depot, built in 1909 at a cost of $300,000, is a striking monument to the importance of railroads in the settling of the West. The slate-shingle mansard roof sets a distinctive French Second Empire tone for the exterior. Inside, Western-theme murals and stained-glass windows create a setting rich with color and texture. *South Temple and 400 West Sts.*

CAPITOL HILL AND THE UNIVERSITY OF UTAH
A Good Tour

To the north and within walking distance of downtown is the **UTAH STATE CAPITOL** ⑰, one of the nation's finest examples of Renaissance Revival architecture. Also on Capitol Hill is the **PIONEER MEMORIAL MUSEUM** ⑱. Northwest of Capitol Hill are the small Victorian homes of the **MARMALADE HILL HISTORIC DISTRICT** ⑲. The next stops are best reached by car. About 10 blocks south of Capitol Hill to 600 South, then six blocks east on 700 East Street, is another of the town's historical treasures, **TROLLEY SQUARE** ⑳, now a shopping, restaurant, and entertainment complex. From here, head south on 700 East to 900 South Street to the expansive Liberty Park and the **TRACY AVIARY** ㉑. Continue east on 900 South Street and then turn north on 1300 East to reach the campus of the University of Utah, with its **UTAH MUSEUM OF NATURAL HISTORY** ㉒ and **UTAH MUSEUM OF FINE ART** ㉓.

Even Way Back, the Backers Were Bakers

Baker's blood has run through the Backers' veins for centuries, and **MRS. BACKER'S PASTRY SHOP** (432 E. South Temple St., tel. 801/532–2022) has been serving grateful customers in Salt Lake City for 75 years. The family is one of many in Salt Lake that came to America to start a new life. Henriette and Gerhard Backer arrived here after fleeing from Germany's political unrest after World War I. Their son and the present owner, Martin, can remember selling bread for a nickel a loaf from a wagon he lugged up the steep streets of the Marmalade Hill District. The family moved into the old Utah governor's mansion on South Temple in 1939. (President Theodore Roosevelt slept in what is now the bakery when the building was the governor's home.)

When you enter the current shop, one whiff tells you that the Backer family has been up since 4 AM producing its trademark meat pies, breads, cookies, and other goodies. Chocolate eclairs are a specialty; they seldom last till the end of the day. More than one generation of brides has bought wedding cakes here (over 22,000 have been sold). The cakes—which take three days to produce, as octogenarian Martin decorates them by hand—could give new couples a little something extra. He met his wife, Phoebe, when she was a young girl working at the counter. They've been married for 60 years, and the longevity of their relationship may bode well for those who buy their cakes.

While modern bakeries often take shortcuts, the Backers still prepare everything—from the custard to the chocolate icing—from scratch. You know that what's on the shelf is fresh. With sons and daughters working alongside them, Martin and Phoebe continue a tradition of both independence and quality.

—By Tom and Gayen Wharton

Next to the University of Utah Medical Center, on the east side of the campus, is **FT. DOUGLAS** ㉔, set up by Union-loyal Westerners to keep an eye on Mormon settlers during the Civil War. Take Connor Road, which begins on the south side of the medical center, for a six-block tour of the complex. Stay on Connor Road for one long block beyond the fort to reach **RED BUTTE GARDEN AND ARBORETUM** ㉕. Past the garden, turn west on Wakara Way, follow it one block to Arapeen Drive, then turn south on Arapeen Drive and follow it for half a mile to Sunnyside Avenue; at Sunnyside Avenue, turn east and continue on for half a mile to **THIS IS THE PLACE HERITAGE PARK** ㉖, which commemorates the Mormons' arrival in Utah. Directly south across Sunnyside Avenue, just east of the state park entrance, is **UTAH'S HOGLE ZOO** ㉗.

TIMING

Though somewhat spread out, the points of interest are in clusters, and their diversity makes for a wonderful way to spend a full day. Try exploring the Capitol Hill attractions in the morning and save Trolley Square for the lunch hour, as it's the most likely spot to find a restaurant or snack bar. Visit the aviary and/or the museums at the University of Utah in the afternoon; fewer students attend in the afternoon than in the morning and parking is more plentiful. Visit the zoo and Red Butte Garden and Arboretum in the late afternoon and watch for the sunset alpenglow on the Wasatch Mountains. Evenings often see special activities at This Is The Place Heritage Park.

What to See

㉔ **FT. DOUGLAS.** Established in 1862, this former military post was established because of strained relations between the U.S. Government and the Mormon settlers. Acting on the assumption that Brigham Young might side with the Confederates during the Civil War, a brigade of California and Nevada Union volunteers was dispatched to this site to keep an eye on things. During their free time, the soldiers took to prospecting in the nearby mountains, which in turn led to the establishment of mining camps like Park City. Today Ft. Douglas showcases several examples of military architecture spread out across manicured grounds. There's also a small military history museum. *East side of Wasatch Blvd. at 300 South St., tel. 801/581–1710, www.fortdouglas.org. Grounds: daily until dusk; museum: Tues.–Sat. noon–4.*

⑲ MARMALADE HILL HISTORIC DISTRICT. So called because its streets were named after fruit trees, this small but interesting neighborhood between 300 and 500 North streets, with Quince Street as its western boundary and Center Street as its eastern one, has been restored thanks to the efforts of the Utah Heritage Foundation. In contrast to most of Salt Lake City's streets, these avenues are steep and narrow. The foundation sells a brochure about the district, including a self-guided tour, for $3.

⑱ PIONEER MEMORIAL MUSEUM. The West's most extensive collection of settlement-era relics, many of which relate to Mormon pioneers, fills 38 rooms—plus a carriage house—on four floors. Displays include clothing, furniture tools, wagons, and carriages. *300 N. Main St., tel. 801/538–1050. Free, but donations accepted. Mon.–Sat. 9–5.*

㉕ RED BUTTE GARDEN AND ARBORETUM. With 25 acres of gardens and 125 undeveloped acres, the grounds provide many pleasurable hours of strolling. Of special interest are the Perennial, Fragrance, and Medicinal gardens, the Daylily Collection, the Water Pavilion, and the Children's Garden. Lectures—on everything from bugs to gardening in arid climates—and concerts are presented regularly. Trails run to areas that were closed to the public for more than a century when Ft. Douglas was manned. The vegetation here was protected, so you get a clear idea of what northern Utah looked like in the early days. The trails also access nearby mountain terrain. *Enter on Wakara Way, east of Foothill Dr., tel. 801/585–0556, www.redbutte.utah.edu. $5. May–Sept., Mon.–Sat. 9–8, Sun. 9–5; Oct.–Apr., Tues.–Sun., 10–5.*

salt lake city vicinity

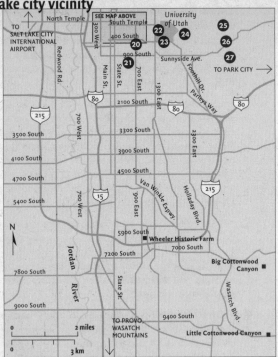

26 THIS IS THE PLACE HERITAGE PARK. Utah's premier historic park includes Old Deseret Village, a re-created 19th-century community. Almost 200 volunteers dressed in period clothing demonstrate what pioneer life was like. You can watch artisans at work in historic buildings, and take carriage rides around the compound. A monument depicts Brigham Young and other Mormon settlers entering the valley that became their home; ringing it are small stone pedestals topped with statues of Native Americans, explorers of the West, and mountain men. 2601 Sunnyside Ave., tel. 801/582–1847, www.parks.state.ut.us/parks/heritage. $6 per vehicle. Daily 7:30 AM–dusk; some special evening activities offered.

21 TRACY AVIARY. Set on 7½ acres, this facility features some 133 species of birds from around the globe: ostriches, bald eagles, flamingos, parrots, several types of waterfowl, and many more. There are two free-flight bird shows daily in summer. 600 E. 900 South St., tel. 801/596–8500, www.tracyaviary.org. $3. Nov.–Mar., daily 9–4:30; Apr.–Oct., daily 9–6.

20 TROLLEY SQUARE. From 1908 to 1945, this sprawling redbrick structure garaged nearly 150 trolleys and electric trains for the Utah Light and Railway Company. In the face of more contemporary modes of transport, however, the facility was closed. In the early 1970s the mission-style edifice was completely overhauled, and today it's one of the West's more intriguing retail centers, with more than 100 boutiques and restaurants. 600 S. 700 East St., tel. 801/521–9877. Mon.–Sat. 10–9, Sun. 12–5.

23 UTAH MUSEUM OF FINE ART. Because it encompasses 74,000 square ft and more than 20 galleries, you'll be glad this facility has a café and a sculpture court—perfect places to rest your weary bones. Special exhibits are mounted regularly, and the vast permanent collection includes Egyptian, Greek, and Roman relics; Italian Renaissance and other European paintings; Chinese ceramics and scrolls; Japanese screens; Thai and Cambodian sculptures; African and Latin American artworks; Navajo rugs; and

American art from the 17th century to the present. *1530 E. South Campus Dr. (a continuation of 400 South St.), just south of Marriott Library, tel. 801/581–7332, www.utah.edu/umfa. Free. Weekdays 10–5, weekends noon–5.*

㉒ UTAH MUSEUM OF NATURAL HISTORY. Anyone who has spent time searching for arrowheads will be well rewarded here. The more than 750,000 pieces—many found during the 1800s—represent almost 3,000 archaeological sites. Exhibits focus on the prehistoric inhabitants of the Colorado Plateau, the Great Basin, and other southwestern locations. Utah's dry climate preserved for centuries not only the structures of these peoples, but also their clothing, foodstuffs, toys, weapons, and ceremonial objects. The aridity preserved dinosaur bones and fossils just as well. In the basement are thousands of specimens, dominated by creatures from the Late Jurassic period, many from the Cleveland-Lloyd quarry. Collections of rocks, minerals, and other fossils round out the museum. Utah wildlife is also well represented, and you can even learn why the state's modern-day residents are so enamored of seagulls. *1340 E. 200 South St., on President's Circle, tel. 801/581–4303, www.umnh.utah.edu. $4. Mon.–Sat. 9:30–5:30, Sun. noon–5.*

㉗ UTAH'S HOGLE ZOO. The zoo houses more than 1,400 animals from all over the world. Most visitors are drawn at once to the polar bear exhibit, where Anana, a cub born here in 2000, stays close to her mother's side. In the primate forest, spider, colobus, and capuchin monkeys romp between an indoor and outdoor area. A children's zoo, interactive exhibits, and special presentations make visits informative and engaging for both adults and children. In summer, youngsters can tour the zoo aboard a miniature train. *2600 E. Sunnyside Ave., tel. 801/582–1631. $7. Daily 9–5.*

⑰ UTAH STATE CAPITOL. In 1912, after the state reaped $800,000 in inheritance taxes from the estate of Union Pacific Railroad president Edward Harriman, work began on the Renaissance Revival structure that tops Capitol Hill. From the exterior steps you get a marvelous view of the entire Salt Lake Valley. Inside, in the rotunda beneath the 165-ft-high dome, is a series of murals depicting the state's history that was commissioned as part of the WPA project during the Depression. Tours not only provide background information about the capitol and its exhibits but also allow you to enter the legislative chambers, the State Reception Room (nicknamed the Gold Room because of its decor), and other areas that are generally off-limits. *Capitol Hill, 400 N. State St., tel. 801/538–3000. Free. Daily 8–8; tours weekdays every ½ hr 9–4.*

OFF THE BEATEN PATH **WHEELER HISTORIC FARM** – Come here to experience 1890s-era farm life by taking an "afternoon chores tour," trying your hand at milking a cow, or riding a draft horse–drawn wagon. *6351 S. 900 East St., tel. 801/264–2212. www.wheelerfarm.com. Free; $1 for special events. Mon.–Sat. 10–5.*

SIDE TRIPS FROM SALT LAKE CITY

Depending on your point of view, the **BINGHAM CANYON COPPER MINE** is either a marvel of human engineering or simply a great big eyesore. This enormous open-pit mine measures nearly 2½ mi across and ½ mi deep—the result of removing 5 billion tons of rock. Since operations began nearly 90 years ago by the Kennecott Utah Copper company, more than 12 million tons of copper have been produced. You can view the mine from an overlook, but be sure to check on hours before making the 22-mi trip here (take I–15 to the 7200 South exit; drive south to 7800 South, then west to Route 48, which leads to the mine). At the visitor center, exhibits and multimedia presentations explain the history and present-day operation of the mine. Outside, trucks the size of dinosaurs and cranes as tall as some apartment buildings continue to reshape the mountain. *Rte. 48, Copperton, tel. 801/252–3234. $2 per vehicle. Apr.–Oct., daily 8–8.*

The Great Salt Lake is eight times saltier than the ocean and second only to the Dead Sea in salinity. What makes it so briny? There's no outlet to the ocean, so salts and other minerals carried by rivers and streams become concentrated in this enormous evaporation pond. Ready access to this wonder is possible at **GREAT SALT LAKE STATE PARK,** 16 mi west of Salt Lake City, on the lake's south shore. (This is primarily a park for bird-watchers and boaters; if you want to test the buoyancy of the water by swimming, try the beaches at Antelope Island State Park.) At the marina, you can make arrangements for group or charter sails. Trips take from one to six hours, and there's a range of reasonable prices to match; some include meals. **SALT ISLAND ADVENTURES** (tel. 801/252–9336, www.gslcruises.com) runs cruises between March and December. *Frontage Rd., 2 mi east of I–80, Exit 104, tel. 801/250–1898. Free. Daily 7 AM–10 PM.*

JORDAN RIVER STATE PARK, a 5-mi riverside walkway accessed from North Temple Street at Redwood Road (1700 West) runs from North Temple Street to 2200 North Street. It has jogging paths, canoeing, picnic facilities, a golf course, and bicycling areas. Like the river in the Middle East for which it's named, Utah's Jordan River runs from fresh water (Utah Lake) to salt (Great Salt Lake). *1084 N. Redwood Rd., Salt Lake City, tel. 801/533–4496. Free. Daily dawn to dusk.*

Calling itself the largest amusement park between Kansas City and the West Coast, **LAGOON** includes all the rides and attractions you'd expect, plus the adjacent Lagoon-A-Beach water park. In operation for more than a century, Lagoon is a Utah landmark. The Sky Scraper, Colossus, and Cliffhanger rides, along with the Pioneer Village and a fine concert series, draw visitors back again and again. Amusement-park veterans can pump up their adrenaline at the X-venture Zone "adventures" that fuse extreme-sports challenges with traditional rides. *375 N. Lagoon Dr., Farmington, 14 mi north of Salt Lake City, Exit 326 off I–15, tel. 801/*

This Lake Is for the Birds

Although it's too salty for fish, the Great Salt Lake teems with algae and bacteria. These provide food for brine shrimp and brine flies, which seem like caviar to the millions of shore birds that stop here during their migrations. Below is a list of some of the more than 250 species that you can spot at natural saltwater marshes, man-made freshwater marshes, and wetland refuges around the lake.

Avocet

Bald Eagle

Black-Necked Stilt

California Gull

Common Snipe

Cormorant

Egret (Great and Snowy varieties)

Grebe (Eared and Western)

Heron (Great Blue and Black-Crowned Night)

Killdeer

Long-Billed Curlew

Long-Billed Dowitcher

Marbled Godwit

Merganser

Northern Phalarope

Plover (Black-Bellied, Lesser, Golden, Snowy, Semipalmated)

Red Knot Sanderling

Sandpiper (Baird's, Least, Pectoral, Semipalmated, Solitary, Spotted, Stilt, Western)

Tern (Caspian and Forster's)

White-Faced Ibis

Willet

Yellowlegs (Greater and Lesser)

—By Tom and Gayen Wharton

451–8000 or 800/748–5246, www.lagoonpark.com. $24–$30. Memorial Day–Labor Day, daily 10 AM–midnight.

From I–15, **ANTELOPE ISLAND STATE PARK** appears to be a deserted, water-bound mountain. In reality, this largest island in Great Salt Lake is home to a variety of wildlife, including a herd of 600 bison descended from a group of 12 animals placed on the island in 1893. In 1983, the lake's level rose dramatically and flooded the 7-mi causeway that leads to the island. The water has since receded, and the 28,000-acre island's beaches, campground, and hiking areas are again accessible. This is the best area to come to for swimming. A concessionaire, **R&G Horseback** (tel. 801/782–4946), rents horses for island explorations. *Rte. 127, Syracuse, 7 mi west of I–15, Exit 335; 30 mi north of Salt Lake City, tel. 801/773–2941. $7 per vehicle, including fee for causeway; $9 camping per night. Daily 7 AM–10 PM.*

EATING OUT

Although there are an increasing number of fine restaurants, some serving ethnic cuisine, the majority of the area's dining establishments are traditional, family-style eateries offering meat and potatoes (and a little fresh fish). Having a drink with dinner is not a problem in the metropolitan and ski-resort restaurants, neither is getting a table at most places. Men might want to wear a jacket at the more expensive establishments, otherwise, dress is casual.

Afghan

$–$$ BABA AFGHAN. This small downtown restaurant has a storefront exterior. Inside, Afghani textiles add color to the walls. Specialties include *poushtee kebab*—grilled lamb marinated in a purée of garlic, onion, and sun-dried grapes, served with balsamic rice caramelized in spices. Weekdays see 20-item buffet lunches. *55 E. 400 South St., tel. 801/596–0786. AE, D, DC, MC, V. Closed Sun.–Mon.*

American

$–$$$ OLD SALT CITY JAIL. Once a brewery, this place has been re-created to resemble an old country jail. The favorites are also old-fashioned: prime rib, chicken, and fish. Reservations are a good idea. *460 S. 1000 East St., tel. 801/359–6090. AE, D, DC, MC, V. No lunch.*

$–$$ COWBOY GRUB. Cowboy paraphernalia—lariats, a mounted buffalo head, spurs, etc.—decorates the room and gets you in the mood for the grub: mostly grilled chicken and steaks, though there's also a salad bar. *2350½ Foothill Blvd., I–80 to Foothill Dr., tel. 801/466–8334. AE, D, DC, MC, V. Closed Sun.*

$–$$ LAMB'S GRILL CAFÉ. Having opened its doors in 1919, Lamb's claims to be Utah's oldest restaurant. The decor is reminiscent of a classy 1930s diner, and this is where most of Salt Lake City's movers and shakers convene for breakfast. The lunch and dinner menus have beef, chicken, and seafood dishes, plus a selection of sandwiches. *169 S. Main St., tel. 801/364–7166. AE, D, DC, MC, V. Closed Sun.*

$–$$ SQUATTER'S PUB BREWERY. It might seem a guilty pleasure to quaff home-brewed beer in such a conservative state as Utah, but that's exactly what's encouraged in this lively pub in the old Boston Hotel. Folks chow down Squatterburgers, Margherita pizza, or huge helpings of fish-and-chips. Anglophiles gravitate to the bread pudding and one of the eight ales on tap. Because it bases production on demand, the pub promises the freshest brew in town. From pale ale to cream stout, no preservatives are used. *147 W. Broadway, tel. 801/363–2739. Reservations not accepted. AE, D, DC, MC, V.*

$ RED BUTTE CAFE. Windows here afford terrific views of the Wasatch Mountains, or you can eat at a picnic table on the patio. The menu has just the right selection of salads, sandwiches, and pastas, with a few southwestern dishes thrown in for good measure. *1414 S. Foothill Blvd., tel. 801/581–9498. AE, D, DC, MC, V.*

salt lake city dining

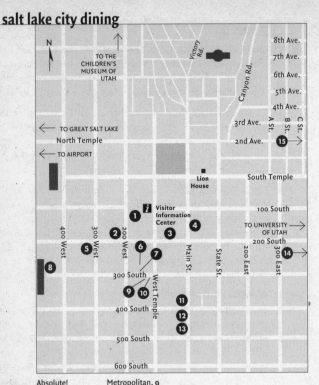

Barbecue

$–$$ SUGAR HOUSE BARBEQUE COMPANY. You place and pick up your order at the counter, then eat it on paper plates with plastic utensils. The food is the real thing, though: authentic Memphis-style dry-rubbed ribs and an array of smoked meats including pulled pork, beef brisket, and turkey breast. Eat out on the patio in nice weather. 2207 S. 700 East St., tel. 801/463–4800. AE, D, DC, MC, V.

Brazilian

$–$$ RODIZIO GRILL. The servers sing here when they're not slicing huge slabs of marinated meat onto your plate. Vegetarians take note: the salad bars here have both Brazilian and American fare; grilled pineapple is a surprise treat. 459 Trolley Sq., tel. 801/220–0500. AE, D, DC, MC, V.

Chinese

$ XIAO LI. The plain wooden tables and white cloth placemats are offset by elaborate Chinese screens and wall hangings. Specialties include shrimp and scallops with mushrooms and garlic sauce. 307 W. 200 South St., tel. 801/328–8688. AE, DC, MC, V. No lunch weekends.

Contemporary

$$$–$$$$ METROPOLITAN. Many Utahns believe there's no finer place to
★ dine than the Metropolitan, whether you feast on wild game or fresh seafood. Try the roasted young chicken with caramelized onions and apple stuffing, sunflower sprouts, and cherry glaze. If you have a hard time choosing just one dish, the bistro area has a tasting menu. Save room for. dessert, though—perhaps rhubarb and strawberry tart with sorbet or caramel soufflé with macadamia sauce. The setting is comfortably urban, the staff has the time and knowledge necessary to make each meal memorable,

salt lake city vicinity dining

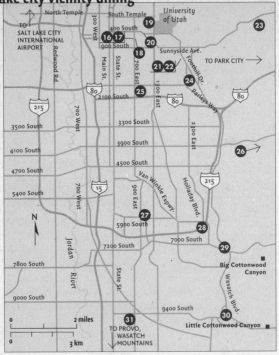

and the live jazz on Saturday night creates a festive atmosphere. *173 W. Broadway, tel. 801/364–3472. AE, D, MC, V.*

$$–$$$$ **LOG HAVEN.** Near the head of Millcreek Canyon, just south of
★ Salt Lake City, this 80-year-old rustic retreat in the pines has lured the likes of Margaret Thatcher and pampered members of the International Olympics Committee for dinner. Chef David Jones fuses the world's finest cuisines into his own unique creations, with dishes influenced by the Pacific Rim, California, the Southwest, and France. Specialties include coriander-rubbed ahi tuna, pepper-seared filet mignon, and Cajun-spiced duck confit. *4 mi up Millcreek Canyon. From I–15, take I–80 East to I–215 South. Take exit for 39th South, turn left at the end of the ramp, left onto Wasatch Blvd., then turn right at 3800 South traffic light, tel. 801/ 272–8255. AE, D, DC, MC, V.*

$ **DESERT EDGE BREWERY.** This lively microbrewery has brass-top tables, loft seating, a sheltered patio, and lots of music and noise. Favorites include coconut rice with grilled chicken, pasta, and salmon. *273 Trolley Sq., tel. 801/521–8917. AE, D, MC, V.*

Continental

$$–$$$$ **THE NEW YORKER AND THE CAFÉ AT THE NEW YORKER.** In the basement of what was once the New York Hotel, built in 1906, this café and dining room has backlit skylights and lots of mirrors. Palm trees are scattered throughout. Seafood is prominent on the menu, but there are also plenty of wild game and beef dishes, all simply prepared. Seating is in booths and tables; the café section is more casual. Reservations are recommended. *60 W. Market St., tel. 801/363–0166. AE, D, DC, MC, V. Closed Sun. No lunch Sat.*

Eclectic

$$–$$$ **ARGENTINE GRILL.** Herb and flower gardens bloom at this comfortable place for much of the year, and during these times be sure to request a table in the glass-enclosed garden room or on the adjoining patio. Specialties include Milanese chicken, salmon with Dijon sauce, double-cut pork chops, and halibut with apricot brandy sauce. 6055 S. 900 East St., tel. 801/265–0205. AE, D, DC, MC, V. Closed Sun.–Mon.

$–$$ OASIS CAFE. An adjacent bookstore, rosy floor tiles, and wide windows create a welcoming environment. There's a good number of pasta and sandwich choices, though the menu also has some seafood dishes. A large beverage selection includes teas, coffees, fresh juices—nothing carbonated, though. 151 S. 500 East St., tel. 801/322–0404. AE, D, DC, MC, V.

$–$$ PORCUPINE PUB AND GRILLE. The decor is modern southwestern chic, but the menu really gets around: cherry-barbecue salmon, Thai chicken, a Portobello mushroom sandwich, tequila lime pasta. Dessert lovers go wild for the chocolate porcupine, a small chocolate cake (shaped like a porcupine, of course) filled with German-chocolate mousse then dipped in milk chocolate, with vanilla-bean ice cream on the side. Beer aficionados will appreciate the pub's 24 brews on tap. 3698 E. Fort Union Blvd., south of downtown at mouth of Big Cottonwood Canyon, tel. 801/942–5555. AE, D, MC, V.

$ CUHINA. This popular eatery is part bakery, part Italian deli, part coffee shop, and part candy store. In nice weather you can dine on the porch with a view of the garden. Scones are a breakfast specialty. Lunch and dinner menus offer such ready-to-eat entrées as meat loaf with garlic potatoes, chicken orzo salad with feta cheese and raisins, or salmon fillets stuffed with cheese and herbs. 1026 E. 2nd Ave., tel. 801/322–3055. MC, V. No dinner Sun.

French

$$$$ LA CAILLE. It's hard to imagine a dining experience more
★ interesting and delectable than the one here. Start with the escargots à la Bourguignonne followed by the wilted-spinach

salad. Then choose from such treats as fresh Norwegian silver salmon baked in parchment or Chateaubriand served with béarnaise sauce and brittle pommes frites. Add personable servers dressed in period costume, the stately surroundings of a replica 18th-century French château, and a 22-acre nature preserve. The result is a dinner worth every penny. *9565 Wasatch Blvd., tel. 801/942–1751. Reservations essential. AE, D, DC, MC, V.*

Italian

$$–$$$$ **BACI TRATTORIA.** A sleek design with a black-marble wraparound bar is the setting for upscale, Italian-inspired food. The specialties include blackened shrimp, scallop and crab fettuccini, and roasted duck in Grand Marnier and orange sauce. A small patio seats 10. *134 W. Pierpont Ave., tel. 801/328–1500. AE, D, DC, MC, V. No lunch Sat. Closed Sun.*

$–$$$ **TUCCANY.** Amid mature trees in a quiet part of the city, Tuscany ★ has six candlelit dining areas, including a cellar and two wrought-iron balconies. The detailed appetizer descriptions deliver what they promise, such as herb-crusted beef carpaccio with caper vinaigrette and shaved Parmesan. The creative entrées include pesto salmon with toasted vegetable couscous. Even more unusual are the manageable slices of a 7-ft chocolate layer cake served in honor of retired Utah Jazz center, Mark Eaton, one of the restaurant's owners. Tuscany also has an outstanding wine list. *2832 E. 6200 South St., tel. 801/277–9919. AE, D, DC, MC, V.*

$–$$ **TUCCI'S.** Don't let the reasonable prices fool you: the food, service, and ambience are far above ordinary. From the chicken breasts topped with shrimp and artichokes to the veal with Portobello mushrooms in Marsala sauce, every dish is bountiful and delicious, and the desserts—try the chocolate mousse—are exquisite. The staff genuinely enjoys providing a pleasant dining experience. A variety of seating areas makes the restaurant suitable for any occasion, from a business lunch or romantic dinner to a casual family meal. 515 S. 700 East St., tel. 801/533-9111. AE, D, DC, MC, V.

Japanese

$–$$ GINZA. In a building that once housed a seedy beer bar, this small downtown restaurant is clean and bright, with colorful place settings and fresh flowers year-round. This is a good choice for sushi novices. 209 W. 200 South St., tel. 801/322–2224. AE, D, DC, MC, V. No lunch Sat. Closed Sun.

$–$$ MIKADO. The plain elegance of Japanese decorating prevails here, with long wooden tables adorned only with fresh flowers. The specials include seared ahi tuna and *shichimi* salmon, as well as *soba* noodles sautéed with Asian vegetables. Reservations are advised. 67 W. 100 South St., tel. 801/328–0929. AE, D, DC, MC, V. No lunch Sat. Closed Sun.

Mexican

$ RAFAEL'S. Away from downtown, this modest restaurant is furnished with reproductions of Native American artwork, and has wide windows and quiet corner tables. Favorites include *chile verde* (pork in a green chile sauce) and various types of enchiladas. 889 E. 9400 South St., Sandy, tel. 801/561–4545. D, MC, V. Closed Sun.

$ RIO GRANDE CAFE. A local artist's work decorates the walls and funky music plays on the jukebox. In nice weather eat outside on the patio. Favorites are the cheese enchiladas and the chimichangas. 270 S. Rio Grande St., tel. 801/364–3302. AE, D, MC, V. No lunch Sun.

Scandinavian

$$–$$$$ ABSOLUTE! RESTAURANT AND BRASSERIE. An indoor waterfall sculpture is the backdrop for small tables set on three levels. Specialties include Alaskan salmon chowder, halibut (in season) with creamy Chardonnay sauce, and lingonberry mousse for dessert. 52 W. 200 South St., tel. 801/359–0899. AE, MC, V. No lunch Sat. Closed Sun.

Seafood

$$–$$$$ MARKET STREET BROILER. Sleek black and white tiles with a lot of stainless steel accompany the equally sleek menu. Seating is at a counter and tables or outside on a patio. The signature item is Australian lobster tail, but any fresh seafood grilled over mesquite is also worth a try. 258 S. 1300 East St., tel. 801/583–8808. AE, D, DC, MC, V.

$$–$$$$ MARKET STREET GRILL. Since it's known for its fresh, well-
★ prepared seafood, you can count on every entrée being a winner, but be sure to check the daily fish specials before ordering. The lively restaurant is owned by Gastronomy, Inc., a Salt Lake chain that transforms historic buildings into tasteful dining spots. 48 Market St., tel. 801/322–4668. Reservations not accepted. AE, D, DC, MC, V.

Southwestern

$$ SANTA FE RESTAURANT. Appetizers at this restaurant, in scenic Emigration Canyon, turn up the heat by combining meat or seafood with chiles and fresh salsas. Salads of local baby greens are accompanied by the crunch of pumpkin or pomegranate seeds. Regional entrées, such as Utah rainbow trout, range from mild to hot. The food is plentiful and carefully prepared, and the warm bread served with all meals is outstanding. Brunch is offered on Sunday. 2100 Emigration Canyon, tel. 801/582–5888. AE, D, MC, V.

$–$$ CAFÉ PIERPONT. Tasty southwestern cuisine is served in a family-oriented setting. Children small enough to walk through the wrought-iron cactus at the door eat for free. The menu includes several fajita and enchilada plates, plus plenty of combination options where you can choose from beef, chicken, or seafood.

122 W. Pierpont Ave., tel. 801/364–1222. AE, D, DC, MC, V. No lunch weekends.

Thai

$–$$ BANGKOK THAI. ★ Superb food and excellent service win this restaurant acclaim year after year. Curry, rice and noodle, vegetarian, and vegan dishes are mainstays, and there's a variety of entrées featuring fresh seafood. The spice level of the carefully prepared food ranges from mild to wild and is tailored to suit your taste. 1400 S. Foothill Dr., tel. 801/582–8424 or 888/852–8424. AE, D, DC, MC, V. No lunch Sun.

SHOPPING

Salt Lake's shopping is concentrated downtown as well as in several malls—some of them quite unusual. Good bets include books, Mormon crafts, and Western collectibles. The vicinity of 300 South and 300 East streets has several shops that specialize in antique jewelry, furnishings, art, and knickknacks.

PLAZAS AND MALLS

CROSSROADS PLAZA (50 S. Main St., tel. 801/531–1799) is an all-inclusive downtown shopping experience. Among its 140 stores and restaurants are Nordstrom and Mervyn's.

East of I–15 in the south end of the city, **FACTORY STORES OF AMERICA** (12101 S. Factory Outlet Dr., tel. 801/571–2933) offers outlet discounts on everything from cookware and coats to luggage, books, and Doc Martens.

At the behest of Brigham Young, dedicated polygamist Archibald Gardner (11 wives) built a flour mill in 1877. Today you can visit the mill and stroll among over 30 specialty shops in the adjacent **GARDNER VILLAGE** (1100 W. 7800 South St., tel. 801/566–8903). Items for sale include furniture and collectibles.

The wares at **TROLLEY SQUARE** (600 S. 700 East St., tel. 801/521–9877) run the gamut from estate jewelry and designer clothes to bath products, baskets, and saltwater taffy. Stores include Laura Ashley, the Gap, Williams-Sonoma, and Banana Republic.

Founded by Brigham Young in 1868, the Zion's Cooperative Mercantile Institution (ZCMI) was America's first department store. Although the ZCMI stores have now become part of the Meier & Frank chain, the name lives on at the **ZCMI CENTER MALL** (South Temple and Main Sts., tel. 801/321–8745), which dates back to 1902. This thoroughly modern shopping center features over 90 stores, including Eddie Bauer and Godiva. Note that it's closed on Sunday.

ANTIQUES

The accent at **ELEMENTÉ** (353 W. Pierpont Ave., tel. 801/355–7400) is on unique and unusual period pieces. Look for bargains in the basement Just a short walk from downtown is **MORIARTY'S ANTIQUES & CURIOSITIES** (959 S. West Temple St., tel. 801/521–7207), which specializes in furnishings for the home and garden. The staff will ship gifts nationwide. Visit **R. M. KENNARD ANTIQUES** (65 W. 300 South St., tel. 801/328–9796) in the heart of downtown for fine American and European art, furniture, and dishes.

BOOKS

DESERET BOOK (36 S. State St., tel. 801/321–8745), purveyor of books and materials related to the Mormon church and its doctrine, has several Salt Lake locations, the largest of which is in the ZCMI Center. In a rambling house with room after room packed with books, **THE KING'S ENGLISH** (1511 S. 1500 East St., tel. 801/484–9100) is a great place to browse. **SAM WELLER'S ZION BOOK STORE** (254 S. Main St., tel. 801/328–2586 or 800/333–7269) stocks more than half a million new and used books.

Crafts Culture

When the Mormons arrived in the Salt Lake Valley, the Church's women formed a group called the Relief Society. They gathered regularly to discuss religion and family, and their hands were never idle during these meetings. Many a quilt or other piece of handwork was created while chatting.

Through the decades, the faces in Relief Society have changed but their focus on family and handicrafts has not. The Mormon Church encourages mothers to stay home, so producing and selling crafts is a great way for them to make extra cash. For more than 60 years a store called Mormon Handicraft has provided crafts supplies and served as an outlet for finished work.

There are so many area craftspeople that the store's buyers have room for only the best quilts, porcelain dolls, baby clothes, wooden objects, and other crafts. You'll also find honey (the state's symbol is a beehive) and saltwater taffy (in honor of the Great Salt Lake).

Although the Church no longer owns or operates the store, it retains a Mormon feel. You can see an upscale Mormon pioneer home—all hardwoods and antiques—with a picture of Brigham Young over the mantel. Rolls, bread, and cookies made fresh daily at the Lion House, Young's historic home, are also for sale. Such baked goods go well with a traditional root beer or sarsaparilla.

—By Tom and Gayen Wharton

CRAFTS

MORMON HANDICRAFT (Main St. at South Temple St., tel. 801/ 355–2141 or 800/843–1480) sells exquisite children's clothing as well as quilts and other crafts—all made by Utah residents. **THE QUILTED BEAR** (145 W. 7200 South St., tel. 801/566–5454) is a co-op with gifts, home accessories, and collectibles created by more than 600 different craftspeople.

OUTDOOR ACTIVITIES AND SPORTS

Salt Lake City is a gateway to the excellent ski resorts strung along the Wasatch Range. There are also a handful of nearby golf courses. In town you can readily bicycle or run along wide streets and through parks, or catch an NBA or WNBA game.

Participant Sports

CYCLING

Salt Lake City is a comparatively easy city to tour by bicycle, thanks to its extra-wide streets and not-so-frenetic traffic. An especially good route is **CITY CREEK CANYON,** east of the capitol. On odd-number days from mid-May through September the road is closed to motor vehicles. Liberty Park, Sugarhouse Park, and Jordan River State Park also have good cycling and running paths.

GOLF

Less than five minutes from downtown you can tee off at the 18-hole **ROSE PARK GOLF COURSE** (1386 N. Redwood Rd., tel. 801/ 596–5030). A championship course and spectacular scenery await you at the **SOUTH MOUNTAIN GOLF CLUB** (1247 E. Rambling Rd., Draper, tel. 801/495–0500). **STONEBRIDGE GOLF CLUB** (4415 Links Dr., West Valley City, tel. 801/908–7888) is a five-minute drive from Salt Lake International Airport, and it offers a Johnny Miller signature design course. If you're near the east bench of the city, try the **UNIVERSITY OF UTAH GOLF COURSE** (102 Fieldhouse Dr., tel. 801/581–6511).

SKIING

Advance equipment and clothing rental reservations are available from **UTAH SKI&GOLF** (134 W. 600 South St., tel. 801/355–9088 or 801/539–8660, www.utahskigolf.com). The company has locations downtown and at Salt Lake International Airport. It also offers free shuttle service from downtown hotels to their stores.

Spectator Sports

BASEBALL

The Pacific Coast League, Triple-A **SALT LAKE STINGERS** (77 W. 1300 South St., tel. 801/485–3800) play at Franklin Covey Field, which has the Wasatch Range for a backdrop.

BASKETBALL

The **UTAH JAZZ** (301 W. South Temple St., tel. 801/355–3865) is Salt Lake's NBA team and a real crowd-pleaser. Home games are played at the Delta Center. The WNBA **UTAH STARZZ** (301 W. South Temple St., tel. 801/358–7328) share the Delta Center with the Utah Jazz.

HOCKEY

Turner Cup Champions for 1995 and 1996, the **UTAH GRIZZLIES** (3200 S. Decker Lake Dr., West Valley City, tel. 801/988–8000) play IHL hockey on the E Center ice.

NIGHTLIFE AND THE ARTS

NIGHTLIFE
Bars and Lounges

The **BAY** (404 S. West Temple St., tel. 801/363–2623) is a smoke- and alcohol-free club with three dance floors. **HARD ROCK CAFE** (505 S. 600 East St., tel. 801/532–7625) features burgers and rock 'n' roll memories. A good place for spotting Utah Jazz basketball players and their visiting competitors is **PORT O'**

Utah's Dynamic Duo

Picture some of the great pairs of all time. Think Batman and Robin, Crosby and Hope, Martin and Lewis. None have anything on Utah Jazz teammates John Stockton and Karl Malone. Together, they own some of the National Basketball Association's most prestigious records. "Stockton-to-Malone" has almost become a cliché because the two members of the original Olympic Dream Team frequently work together to confound opponents with the basic "pick and roll" play.

The 6'1" Stockton, who played college ball at tiny Gonzaga in Spokane, Washington, holds NBA records for assists and steals. He has also played more games for the same franchise than any athlete in league history. Though one of the smallest NBA players, the 175-pound guard's pinpoint passing and ability to steal the ball make him one of the most respected. The father of six children is a quiet family man who reveals little about his life off the court.

Malone, a 6'9", 256-pound native of Summerfield, Louisiana, has grabbed more than 13,000 rebounds and scored over 32,000 points, making him second only to Kareem Abdul-Jabbar in career points. He played 1,273 of 1,280 games in his first 16 years in the league. This means that the two-time most valuable league player has racked up more minutes on the court than all but three players in NBA history. He's also the only player ever named to the All-NBA first team 11 times. Nicknamed The Mailman because he delivers so often, Malone is an avid outdoorsman. He created the Karl Malone Foundation for Kids to help children in the Intermountain West.

—By Tom and Gayen Wharton

CALL (78 W. 400 South St., tel. 801/521–0589), a sports bar with 14 satellite dishes and 26 TVs.

Nightclubs

The **DEAD GOAT SALOON** (165 S. West Temple St., tel. 801/328–4628) features live music nightly. The tempo is upbeat, and the grill is fired up for lunch and dinner. **GREEN STREET SOCIAL CLUB** (602 E. 500 South St., tel. 801/532–4200) is a fine spot to meet or make friends while enjoying light food, live music, and dancing. The art deco **ZEPHYR CLUB** (301 S. West Temple St., tel. 801/355–5646) showcases both local and nationally recognized bands.

THE ARTS
Dance

Salt Lake's three main dance companies perform at the historic **CAPITOL THEATRE** (50 W. 200 South St., tel. 801/355–2787). **BALLET WEST** (tel. 801/355–2787) is considered one of the nation's top ballet companies, performing both classical and original works. **REPERTORY DANCE THEATRE** (tel. 801/534–1000) presents modern-dance performances. **RIRIE-WOODBURY DANCE COMPANY** (tel. 801/328–1062) is Salt Lake's premier modern-dance troupe. It's recognized for its innovation and commitment to community education.

Music

You can hear the **MORMON TABERNACLE CHOIR** (Temple Sq., tel. 801/240–2534) in the Tabernacle on Sunday morning at 9:30 (be seated by 9:15) or during rehearsals on Thursday at 8 PM. The choir, which includes men and women of all ages from around the Intermountain region, performs sacred music, with some secular—classical and patriotic—works.

The **UTAH SYMPHONY** (123 W. South Temple St., tel. 801/533–6683) performs 260 concerts annually, both at home in the

Salt Lake and Its Spirits

Utah repealed Prohibition in February 1933. In fact, it can be considered the state responsible for ending national prohibition, because it was the 36th, and final state to ratify the 21st Amendment. Still, the rumor persists that it's impossible to get a drink in Utah. Not so—it just requires a little information.

State-operated liquor stores sell bottled liquor and wine. Beer is available at most grocery stores. In general, state stores are inside another business such as a convenience store; they may consist merely of a window next to which a list of merchandise and prices is posted. Throughout the state, the police can cite you for having a bottle of liquor or wine without the State Liquor Authority sticker on it, so it's best not to bring liquor into Utah with you.

If you want to have a drink with a meal, call ahead to be sure that your restaurant of choice serves alcohol (particularly in rural areas). Whether or not alcohol is available will be based on local laws or the whims of the restaurant. In some places your server can bring you a drink but isn't supposed to ask if you want one. In such cases, simply ask to see the beverage menu once you're seated. You can also buy drinks in bars known legally as "non-exclusive private clubs." You need only purchase a temporary membership for a small fee.

acoustically acclaimed Maurice Abravanel Concert Hall and in cities across the nation and abroad.

Opera

UTAH OPERA COMPANY (Capitol Theatre, 50 W. 200 South St., tel. 801/355–2787) produces four operas a year, which often feature nationally recognized stars.

Theater

OFF BROADWAY THEATRE (272 S. Main St., tel. 801/355–4628) puts on musicals, plays, and improvisational comedy events. **PIONEER THEATRE COMPANY** (300 S. 1400 East St., tel. 801/581–6961) features classic and contemporary musicals and plays during its season, which runs from September through May. **SALT LAKE ACTING COMPANY** (168 W. 500 North St., tel. 801/363–7522) is recognized for its development of new plays. Performances run year-round.

WHERE TO STAY

Although chains are ubiquitous, there's still a great variety of accommodations, from the tall, modern, downtown business hotels to historic bed-and-breakfasts to modest motels that simply provide a good place to rest after a day of sightseeing.

$$$$ **GRAND AMERICA.** More a destination than a place to spend the
★ night, this 24-story white-granite hotel sits on 20 acres. Its gardens, pools, shops, ballrooms, and meeting rooms nearly make up a small village. Throughout, English wool carpets, French furniture and tapestries, Italian marble, Irish crystal, and Spanish stonework demonstrate that quality, elegance, and the beauty of natural materials are still valued. Original art hangs everywhere, making a stroll around the building a pleasant way to pass an afternoon. Guest rooms are charming and spacious, and include high-speed T1 data ports. 555 S. Main St., 84111, tel. 801/258–6000 or 800/621–4505, fax 801/258–6911, www.

grandamerica.com. 810 rooms. 2 restaurants, lounge, in-room data ports, in-room safes, refrigerators, room service, 3 pools, sauna, spa, health club, shops, laundry service, concierge floor, business services, convention center, meeting rooms, airport shuttle, free parking. AE, D, DC, MC, V.

$$$–$$$$ WOLFE KREST BED & BREAKFAST. A Capitol Hill landmark, this stately Georgian Revival manor epitomizes elegance—inside and out. Rooms are individually decorated; some have such touches as four-poster beds and seats tucked into bay windows, and all have fireplaces and Jacuzzis. Take in the sunrise from the patio or spend an afternoon relaxing in one of the many lounge areas. *273 N. E. Capitol Blvd., 84103, tel. 801/521–8710 or 800/669–4525, fax 801/531–0522, www.wolfekrest.com. 13 rooms. Dining room, in-room VCRs, meeting room. AE, D, DC, MC, V. BP.*

$$–$$$$ ANNIVERSARY INN AT KAHN MANSION. This Victorian-style mansion is famed for its over-the-top theme rooms. The Kahn Mansion and Country Villa suites are among the more traditional ones. If you're more adventurous, request the Tom Sawyer Room (the bed is on a log raft), the Jackson Hole Suite (the bed is in a covered wagon), or the Fisherman's Wharf Suite (with a ship bed and a cavelike bathroom). All rooms have jetted two-person tubs. *678 E. South Temple St., 84102, tel. 801/363–4900, fax 801/328–9955, www.anniversaryinn.com. 14 rooms. In-room VCRs. AE, D, DC, MC, V. CP.*

$$–$$$$ INN AT TEMPLE SQUARE. A nice alternative to the chains, this seven-story downtown brick hotel is across the street from the Salt Palace convention center. Rooms (all are no-smoking) have a 1930s style and floral wallpaper; some have chaises longues on which to drape yourself like an Erté figure. The high-ceilinged lobby has a chandelier and fireplace. *71 W. South Temple St., 84101, tel. 801/531–1000 or 800/843–4668, fax 801/536–7272, www.theinn.com. 90 rooms, 10 suites. Restaurant, room service, business services, airport shuttle. AE, D, DC, MC, V. CP.*

salt lake city lodging

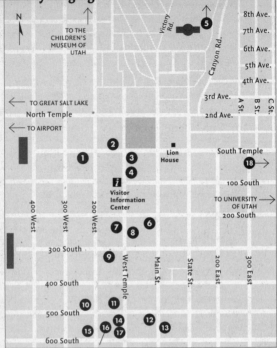

N

TO THE CHILDREN'S MUSEUM OF UTAH

TO GREAT SALT LAKE

North Temple

TO AIRPORT

Victory Rd.

Canyon Rd.

8th Ave.
7th Ave.
6th Ave.
5th Ave.
4th Ave.

3rd Ave.
2nd Ave.

A St.
B St.
C St.

Lion House

South Temple

100 South

TO UNIVERSITY OF UTAH
200 South

Visitor Information Center

400 West
300 West
200 West
West Temple
Main St.
State St.
200 East
300 East

300 South

400 South

500 South

600 South

$$–$$$$ **LA EUROPA ROYALE.** On a wooded lot in South Salt Lake, this
★ small, elegant hotel pampers its guests. The two landscaped
acres invite after-meal walks. There's easy access to the resorts
in Big and Little Cottonwood Canyons and individual ski lockers
are on the property. Guest rooms are individually decorated
but not fussy. Each has a gas fireplace, a Jacuzzi, a data-grade
phone system, a data port, and a desk. The complimentary sit-
down breakfasts are creative and well prepared. *1135 E. Vine St.,
84121, tel. 801/263-7999 or 800/523-8767, fax 801/263-8090,
www.laeuropa.com. 8 rooms. Dining room, in-room data ports, gym,
laundry service and dry cleaning, airport shuttle. AE, D, DC, MC, V. BP.*

$$$ **CHASE SUITE HOTEL.** These airy and spacious suites have vaulted
ceilings, fireplaces, full kitchens, and sitting areas. The folks
here seem to want you to keep in touch: each suite has two
phones, two TVs, high-speed Internet access, and free videos. Only
30 minutes from most ski facilities, the hotel can be an alternative
to pricey all-suite lodging at the resorts. Small pets are allowed,
though there's a $5 per-day surcharge and a $50 nonrefundable
deposit. *765 E. 400 South St., 84102, tel. 801/532-5511 or 888/433-
6071, fax 801/531-0416, www.woodfinsuitehotels.com. 126 suites. In-
room VCRs, pool, hot tub, meeting rooms, airport shuttle. AE, D, DC, MC,
V. BP.*

$$$ **MARRIOTT HOTEL.** Large and convenient, this chain hotel has
spacious rooms and a lovely indoor pool. A stay here puts you close
to the Salt Palace convention center and the Crossroads Mall and
just half a block from Temple Square. *75 S. West Temple St., 84101,
tel. 801/531-0800, fax 801/532-4127. www.marriott.com. 515 rooms.
Restaurant, in-room data ports, room service, indoor-outdoor pool, hot
tub, health club, coin laundry, dry cleaning, business services, airport shuttle.
AE, D, DC, MC, V.*

$$–$$$ **ARMSTRONG MANSION.** Trees and hedges adorn the front yard
of this brick Victorian mansion. The themed rooms are named
for the months and decorated in a subtly seasonal style December
Dreams has dark green and dark red walls, a brass bed, and a

salt lake city vicinity lodging

Anton Boxrud Bed & Breakfast, 19

Armstrong Mansion, 20

Brigham Street Inn, 21

Chase Suite Hotel, 23

Comfort Inn, 35

Comfort Inn Airport, 26

Courtyard by Marriott, 36

Days Inn Airport, 25

La Europa Royale, 33

Hampton Inn Salt Lake City–North, 27

Hampton Inn–Sandy, 37

Holiday Inn–Downtown, 29

Quality Inn–Midvalley, 31

La Quinta, 34

Radisson Hotel Airport, 28

Reston Hotel, 32

Saltair Bed & Breakfast, 22

Sleep Inn, 38

University Park Marriott, 24

Wildflowers Bed & Breakfast, 30

fireplace. The March room is all fresh and elegant whites, down to the gauze hung over the bed. Note that smoking is prohibited everywhere in the inn. Restaurants, shopping, and Temple Square are close. *667 E. 100 South St., 84102, tel. 801/531–1333 or 800/708–1333, fax 801/531–0282, www.armstrong-bb.com. 13 rooms. In-room VCRs. AE, D, DC, MC, V. BP.*

$$–$$$ HILTON–SALT LAKE CITY CENTER. Once a Doubletree, this Hilton is still one of the city's largest and best-appointed places to stay. It's within walking distance of many downtown attractions and great restaurants, yet it also caters to skiers by offering complimentary ski storage. *255 S. West Temple St., 84101, tel. 801/328–2000, fax 801/532–1953. 499 rooms. 2 restaurants, bar, pool, massage, sauna, health club, free parking. AE, D, DC, MC, V.*

$$–$$$ HOTEL MONACO SALT LAKE CITY. This downtown hotel is ensconced in the former Continental Bank Building, with its classical cornices, cartouches, and carved stone faces of Norse gods. Inside, the 1940s Hollywood atmosphere is casually elegant, upbeat, and fun. Early evening gatherings in the lobby give you a chance to mingle with other guests next to the fire, or to receive a head, neck, or back massage in a quiet corner of the lobby that's set up as a sultan's tent. Amenities for skiers include ski storage and transportation to the slopes. For a small fee you can participate in a variety of outings, with all equipment and transportation provided. There's even an unusual program that allows you to adopt a goldfish during your stay. *15 W. 200 South St., 84101, tel. 801/595–0000 or 877/294–9710, fax 801/532–8500, www.monaco-saltlakecity.com. 187 rooms, 38 suites. Restaurant, bar, in-room data ports, room service, health club, laundry service, meeting room, free parking. AE, D, DC, MC, V.*

$$–$$$ LITTLE AMERICA HOTEL. Inside this 17-story hotel are such
★ niceties as lobby fireplaces, brass railings, chandeliers, and marble tubs. Guest rooms are elegant, with textured fabrics,

plush seating, and variable lighting. *500 S. Main St., 84101, tel. 801/ 363–6781 or 800/453–9450, fax 801/596–5911, www.littleamerica. com. 850 rooms. Restaurant, coffee shop, piano bar, room service, indoor-outdoor pool, hot tub, sauna, health club, coin laundry, dry cleaning, laundry service, business services, airport shuttle, free parking. AE, D, DC, MC, V.*

$$–$$$ SALTAIR BED & BREAKFAST. Sitting with a book before a roaring fire in the formal parlor of this 1903 Victorian home is the perfect way to end the day. Rooms have fine oak woodwork and period antiques. Suites with fireplaces and kitchens are available, and families or groups can stay in one of the small separate houses on the property. Breakfast, which features hearty American fare, is served in the dining room. *164 S. 900 East St., 84102, tel. 801/ 533–8184 or 800/733–8184, fax 801/595–0332, www.saltlakebandb. com. 7 rooms, 9 suites. Dining room, kitchenettes (some), free parking. AE, D, DC, MC, V. BP.*

$$ ANTON BOXRUD BED & BREAKFAST. Quirky furnishings— some of them antiques—from all over the world fill the rooms of this elegant, yet casual, Victorian manor just a 15-minute stroll from the city center. The complimentary evening snacks and beverages served near the parlor's bay window are as delicious as the bountiful breakfasts served in the dining room. *57 S. 600 East St., 84102, tel. 801/363–8035 or 800/524–5511, fax 801/596–1316, www.bbiu.org/antonboxrud. 7 rooms. Dining room, hot tub. AE, D, DC, MC, V. BP.*

$$ BEST WESTERN-SALT LAKE PLAZA. Within walking distance of shopping, restaurants, Temple Square, and the Delta Center, this is a good place to stay if you are interested in the city's history and culture. *122 W. South Temple St., 84101, tel. 801/521–0130, fax 801/322–5057, www.plaza-hotel.com. 226 rooms. Restaurant, in-room data ports, room service, pool, hot tub, gym, coin laundry, dry cleaning, business services, airport shuttle. AE, D, DC, MC, V.*

$$ BRIGHAM STREET INN. If you love historic B&Bs, this is the place to stay. This turn-of-the-20th-century mansion was carefully restored by Salt Lake architect John Pace. Each of the superbly appointed guest rooms was decorated by a different interior designer. Some are done in pastels, with the visual focus being the inn's large tree-shaded windows; others offer jewel-tone upholstery and recessed lighting; most have king-size beds and fireplaces. The original woodwork has been preserved throughout. The breakfast is Continental. *1135 E. South Temple St., 84102, tel. 801/364–4461 or 800/417–4461, fax 801/521–3201, www.brighamstreetinn.citysearch.com. 9 rooms. Breakfast room. AE, D, DC, MC, V. CP.*

$$ COURTYARD BY MARRIOTT. The large desks with data ports and spacious work areas were designed for business travelers. But shoppers should take note: the hotel is a standout in a cluster of properties just off I–15 and next to a factory outlet mall. *10701 Holiday Park Dr., Sandy, 84070, tel. 801/571–3600, fax 801/572–1383, www.courtyard.com. 117 rooms, 7 suites. Restaurant, bar, in-room data ports, room service, indoor pool, hot tub, health club, coin laundry, laundry service, business services. AE, D, DC, MC, V.*

$$ CRYSTAL INN. Two blocks from Temple Square, this four-story property is close to restaurants and offices. The spacious rooms include sitting and work areas, and you can get a second phone line if you need one. *230 W. 500 South St., 84101, tel. 801/328–4466 or 800/366–4466, fax 801/328–4072, www.crystalinns.com. 159 rooms, 16 suites. In-room data ports, indoor pool, hot tub, health club, coin laundry, dry cleaning, airport shuttle. AE, D, DC, MC, V. BP.*

$$ EMBASSY SUITES. The entrance strikes a cool, relaxing note, and the suites are spacious. A stay here puts you close to restaurants, shopping, and LDS Church facilities. *110 W. 600 South St., 84301, tel. 801/359–7800, fax 801/359–3753, www.embassysuites.com. 241 suites. Restaurant, in-room data ports, indoor pool, hot tub, health club, coin laundry, business services, airport shuttle. AE, D, DC, MC, V. BP.*

$$ HAMPTON INN–SANDY. Pleasant rooms, nice furnishings, and a moderate price make this a worthy choice. It's close to I–15, and there are movie theaters, restaurants, and a shopping mall within a mile. 10690 S. Holiday Park Dr., Sandy 84070, tel. 801/571–0800, fax 801/572–0708. 131 rooms. Indoor pool, hot tub, coin laundry. AE, D, DC, MC, V.

$$ PEERY HOTEL. Everything smacks of late-19th-century sophistication—except maybe the modest prices. In the lobby the marble floors, brass chandeliers, and grand piano are polished to perfection. Rooms have beige and gold spreads and drapes with subdued yet stately patterns. Pristine white sheers are hung on windows and draped canopy-style above the heads of beds. Highly polished wood bureaus or desks—some of them period pieces—and the occasional chair or settee upholstered in aubergine or rose add touches of color. The in-room and on-site amenities are as abundant as the decor is classy. 110 W. 300 South St., 84101, tel. 801/521–4300 or 800/331–0073, fax 801/575–5014, www.peeryhotel.com. 73 rooms. 2 restaurants, bar, pizzeria, in-room data ports, room service, no-smoking rooms, hot tub, health club, business services, airport shuttle. AE, D, DC, MC, V. CP.

$$ QUALITY INN–MIDVALLEY. Although it's not posh, this two-story motel is affordable, tidy, and nicely appointed. Each of its large rooms has a desk. It's about 15 minutes from downtown, and the interstate is within easy reach. 4465 Century Dr., 84123, tel. 801/268–2533, fax 801/266–6206, www.qualityinn.com. 132 rooms. In-room data ports, pool, hot tub, coin laundry, business services, airport shuttle. AE, D, DC, MC, V. CP.

$$ RADISSON HOTEL AIRPORT. This very comfortable hotel is your best lodging bet near the airport. Rooms include a wet bar and refrigerator, and there's a complimentary Continental breakfast. 2177 W. North Temple St., 84116, tel. 801/364–5800, fax 801/364–5823, www.radisson.com. 127 rooms. Restaurant, refrigerators, pool, hot tub, exercise room, airport shuttle. AE, D, DC, MC, V. CP.

$$ SHERATON SALT LAKE CITY. A full-service hotel and convention center in the heart of town, the Sheraton has a huge lobby, with oversize chairs and fireplace, and spacious rooms, some with balconies. Perks include newspapers and coffee in the morning. 150 W. 500 South St., 84101, tel. 801/532–3344 or 800/421–7602, fax 801/531–0705. 270 rooms, 50 suites. Restaurant, bar, in-room data ports, pool, hair salon, hot tub, sauna, gym, business services, meeting rooms. AE, D, DC, MC, V.

$$ SHILO INN. A couple of blocks from Temple Square, this hotel combines the convenience of a downtown location with good rates. Service is reasonable, and the amenities, such as the complimentary breakfast buffet, pool and fitness room, and outside glass elevator that affords a spectacular city view, are much better than you'd expect for the price. 206 S. West Temple St., 84101, tel. 801/521–9500, fax 801/359–6527, www.shiloinns.com. 200 rooms. 2 restaurants, bar, pool, hot tub, sauna, gym, coin laundry, airport shuttle, free parking. AE, D, DC, MC, V. CP.

$$ UNIVERSITY PARK MARRIOTT. Proximity to the Red Butte Garden and Arboretum makes this a good resting place if you're a garden lover. The University of Utah campus is also close, as are restaurants and downtown attractions. 480 Wakara Way, 84108, tel. 801/581–1000, fax 801/584–3321, www.marriott.com. 190 rooms, 28 suites. Restaurant, bar, indoor pool, hot tub, health club, business services, airport shuttle. AE, D, DC, MC, V.

$$ WESTCOAST HOTEL. Close to I–15 exits and refurbished in 1999, this downtown high-rise is within walking distance of the Salt Palace convention center and Delta Center. The top-floor restaurant is popular locally. 161 W. 600 South St., 84111, tel. 801/521–7373, fax 801/524–0378, www.westcoast.com. 389 rooms, 4 suites. Restaurant, coffee shop, room service, pool, hot tub, gym, hair salon, business services, airport shuttle. AE, D, DC, MC, V.

$$ WILDFLOWERS BED & BREAKFAST. An elegant "painted lady" with a private yard, this inn was built in 1891. Although the interior has been renovated to provide more light, the rooms are furnished in keeping with the period. If you're traveling with a group, you can also reserve the full-floor suite that has a full kitchen and dining room. Smoking isn't allowed anywhere on the premises. 936 E. 1700 South St., 84105, tel. 801/466–0600 or 800/569–0009 (reservations), fax 801/466–4728, www.wildflowersbb.com. 5 rooms. AE, D, MC, V. BP.

$$ WYNDHAM HOTEL. Here you're minutes from two malls and Temple Square, close to the Delta Center and Abravanel Hall, and 30 minutes from ski resorts. The rooms are comfortable and have work areas. 215 W. South Temple St., 84101, tel. 801/531–7500, fax 801/328–1289, www.wyndham.com. 371 rooms, 10 suites. Restaurant, bar, in-room data ports, room service, indoor pool, hot tub, health club, dry cleaning, business services, airport shuttle. AE, D, DC, MC, V.

$–$$ COMFORT INN. Location is key here. With easy freeway and resort access, you can readily get things done during your stay, whether that means closing a business deal, hitting the slopes, or shopping in the valley. 8955 S. 255 West St., Sandy, 84070, tel. 801/255–4919, fax 801/255–4998, www.comfortinn.com. 97 rooms. In-room data ports, in-room VCRs, indoor pool, hot tub, business services. AE, D, DC, MC, V. CP.

$–$$ COMFORT INN AIRPORT. The furnishings make this new facility a more upscale property than many in this chain. Some pets are allowed (there's a $15 nonrefundable deposit). 200 N. Admiral Byrd Rd., 84116, tel. 801/537–7444 or 800/535–8742, fax 801/532–4721, www.comfortinn.com. 154 rooms. Restaurant, pool, hot tub, business services, airport shuttle. AE, D, MC, V.

$–$$ DAYS INN AIRPORT. Halfway between downtown and the airport, this renovated hotel has good amenities for both families and business travelers. Some pets are allowed. 1900 W. North Temple St., 84116, tel. 801/539–8538, fax 801/595–1041, www.daysinn.com. 110 rooms. In-room data ports, indoor pool, health club, coin laundry, business services, meeting room, airport shuttle. AE, D, DC, MC, V. CP.

$–$$ HAMPTON INN SALT LAKE CITY–NORTH. This is a good alternative to pricier downtown lodgings, yet still within easy reach of Salt Lake City. Eight miles north of downtown, the five-story hotel is close to businesses and restaurants. Some pets are allowed. *2393 S. 800 West St., Woods Cross 84087, tel. 801/296–1211, fax 801/296–1222, www.cottontree.net/hampton. 57 rooms, 3 suites. In-room data ports, indoor pool, hot tub, coin laundry, laundry service, airport shuttle. AE, D, DC, MC, V. CP.*

$–$$ HOLIDAY INN–DOWNTOWN. The tennis courts are nice extras if you want to stay downtown but still be active. Just south of the major business district, this hotel is convenient to everything, including several nearby restaurants. *999 S. Main St., 84111, tel. 801/359–8600, fax 801/359–7186, www.holiday-inn.com. 292 rooms, 14 suites. Restaurant, bar, indoor-outdoor pool, hot tub, 2 tennis courts, health club, playground, coin laundry, business services, airport shuttle. AE, D, DC, MC, V.*

$–$$ LA QUINTA. A bit south of the city, this is one of the first South Valley motels. Rooms are spacious, with large TVs and desks with data ports. Recent remodeling and new furniture have made everything seem fresh. Some pets are allowed. *7231 S. 440 West St., Midvale 84047, tel. 801/566–3291, fax 801/562–5943, www.laquinta.com. 119 rooms, 2 suites. In-room data ports, indoor pool, hot tub, coin laundry, dry cleaning, business services. AE, D, DC, MC, V. CP.*

$–$$ RAMADA INN–DOWNTOWN. All rooms and facilities ring an enclosed courtyard in this downtown hotel, a design that makes for truly pleasant stays. The courtyard's casual, tropical atmosphere is created by a pool and hot tub, several garden-like seating areas, large plants, and cages of finches and parakeets. The rooms are clean and airy, and the amenities—fitness center, billiards, sauna, lounge—combined with the reasonable price might make you want to stay an extra day. Some pets are allowed, though there's a $10 fee for this. *230 W. 600 South St., 84103, tel. 801/364–5200, fax 801/364–0974, www.ramadainnslc.com. 120 rooms.*

Hotel How-Tos

Where you stay does make a difference. Do you prefer a modern high-rise or an intimate B&B? A center-city location or the quiet suburbs? What facilities do you want? Sort through your priorities, then price it all out.

HOW TO GET A DEAL After you've chosen a likely candidate or two, phone them directly and price a room for your travel dates. Then call the hotel's toll-free number and ask the same questions. Also try consolidators and hotel-room discounters. You won't hear the same rates twice. On the spot, make a reservation as soon as you are quoted a price you want to pay.

PROMISES, PROMISES If you have special requests, make them when you reserve. Get written confirmation of any promises.

SETTLE IN Upon arriving, make sure everything works—lights and lamps, TV and radio, sink, tub, shower, and anything else that matters. Report any problems immediately. And don't wait until you need extra pillows or blankets or an ironing board to call housekeeping. Also check out the fire emergency instructions. Know where to find the fire exits, and make sure your companions do, too.

IF YOU NEED TO COMPLAIN Be polite but firm. Explain the problem to the person in charge. Suggest a course of action. If you aren't satisfied, repeat your requests to the manager. Document everything: Take pictures and keep a written record of who you've spoken with, when, and what was said. Contact your travel agent, if he made the reservations.

KNOW THE SCORE When you go out, take your hotel's business cards (one for everyone in your party). If you have extras, you can give them out to new acquaintances who want to call you.

TIP UP FRONT For special services, a tip or partial tip in advance can work wonders.

USE ALL THE HOTEL RESOURCES A concierge can make difficult things easy. But a desk clerk, bellhop, or other hotel employee who's friendly, smart, and ambitious can often steer you straight as well. A gratuity is in order if the advice is helpful.

Restaurant, bar, pool, sauna, health club, hot tub, recreation room, coin laundry, laundry services, meetings rooms, airport shuttle, free parking. AE, D, DC, MC, V.

$–$$ RESTON HOTEL. Just 10 minutes from downtown and 15 minutes from the airport, this three-story hotel has more than you'd expect from a budget property. Take a swim in the indoor pool or relax in the hot tub. The café serves a complimentary Continental breakfast. *5335 College Dr., Murray 84123, tel. 801/264–1054 or 800/231–9710, fax 801/264–1054, www.restonhotelslc.com. 98 rooms. Café, indoor pool, hot tub, meeting rooms. AE, D, DC, MC, V. CP.*

$ SLEEP INN. The setting, appropriately enough given the hotel's name, is in the quiet southwest end of the valley near the Jordan River Mormon Temple. Rooms have comfortable sitting areas and supersize showers. *10676 S. 300 West St., South Jordan 84095, tel. 801/572–2020, fax 801/572–2459. www.utahhospitality.com. 68 rooms, shower only. In-room data ports, in-room VCRs, indoor pool, coin laundry, business services. AE, D, DC, MC, V. CP.*

$ TRAVELODGE CITY CENTER. Rooms are plain but comfortable, and were given face-lifts in 2000. It's just off an I–15 exit and convenient to downtown. *524 S. West Temple St., 84101, tel. 801/531–7100, fax 801/359–3814, www.travelodge.com. 60 rooms. Pool, hot tub, business services. AE, D, DC, MC, V. CP.*

Although its landscape is crisscrossed by freeways and dappled by towns large and small, the vast Wasatch Front still beckons adventurers with its alpine forests and windswept canyons. Those who visit follow in the footsteps of Native Americans and in the wagon ruts of Mormon pioneers and miners.

In This Chapter

Updated by Kate Boyes

the wasatch front

IMAGINE WAKING EACH DAY TO A MOUNTAIN VIEW with peaks that rise to more than 11,000 ft. That's just what the residents of Salt Lake City, Ogden, Logan, Provo, and other Utah communities do. The Wasatch Range, which stretches some 160 mi from the Idaho border to central Utah, is a complex assemblage of igneous, sedimentary, and metamorphic formations. Its western base— a corridor known as the Wasatch Front—is home to three-fourths of all Utahns. And both the range and the front make up one of the nation's premier mountain playgrounds.

Uppermost in many people's minds is the legendary skiing found at resorts such as Snowbird, Alta, and Park City. But this region is truly a year-round destination. Bright-blue lakes at state park facilities afford fantastic boating, sailing, windsurfing, and waterskiing opportunities. Add to this picturesque mountain communities, miles of hiking and biking trails, and truly spectacular alpine scenery, and you have a vacation that's hard to beat.

Numbers in the margin correspond to points of interest on The Wasatch Front map.

ALTA

❶ *28 mi from Salt Lake City via I–15 south, I–215 east, and Rte. 210 south.*

Within Little Cottonwood Canyon, the nation's second-oldest ski area started in the 1800s as a silver-mining camp. So frenzied was the pace back then that the year-round population topped

The Front and Its Faults

The geology of the Wasatch Mountains gives the Salt Lake Valley its character. Few places in the world can show off such distinct geologic features in as small an area as the 50 to 70 miles along the Wasatch Front. One section, from City Creek Canyon in the north to Bells Canyon in the south, has 10 distinct geologic zones. Each canyon has a different look, with rocks of varying ages and colors. Glaciers formed some; flowing water created others.

The reddish rocks visible on a drive up Parley's Canyon come from the Jurassic period. Suicide Rock, at the canyon's mouth, dates from the earlier Triassic age. Lower portions of Big Cottonwood Canyon have billion-year-old Precambrian rock. To the south, Little Cottonwood Canyon has comparatively new formations: a molten igneous mass pushed its way almost to the surface a mere 32 million years ago. Granite formed here was used to build the Mormon Temple in Salt Lake.

Tongues of the Wasatch Fault run along the front of the Wasatch Mountains. This fault is where the earth cracks as the Great Basin stretches by a couple of centimeters annually. For this to happen, the valleys from California through to the Wasatch Range must fall slightly. Portions of Salt Lake Valley's Wasatch Boulevard and 1300 East streets are on fault lines. You can tell that you're near a fault when the east–west streets suddenly get steeper. Although geologists say that a quake could happen any time, the valley hasn't experienced a major one in recorded history. Where to grab some dinner should be a bigger concern than being shaken by an earthquake.

–By Tom and Gayen Wharton

8,000. The eventual crash of the silver market left the canyon virtually empty for decades. Then the Alta Lifts Company pieced a lift together using parts from an old mine tram. In January 1939 the ski industry was born.

But skiing isn't all there is to do. Many cycling and hiking trails access the higher reaches of the Wasatch–Cache National Forest from Alta. The trails over Catherine Pass will put you at the head of Big Cottonwood Canyon at the Brighton Ski Area. The hike to Catherine Pass is relatively easy and quite scenic.

The Resort

ALTA is widely acclaimed for both what it has and what it doesn't have. It promises a generous helping of Wasatch powder—up to 500 inches a year. What you won't find is glitz and pomp. Duct tape on ripped nylon pants is Alta chic. The lift system seems antiquated and poorly laid out, trails often flatten out quickly or lead nowhere, and trail signs are rare (only interloping tourists, it seems, don't know their way around). Alta is so retro that it's one of the few ski areas left in the country that disallows snowboarding.

Alta sprawls across two large basins, Albion and Wildcat, comprising mostly open bowls and meadows but with some trail skiing. There are no clear, easily readable fall lines; instead, they drop and roll away in many directions and at many angles. Furthermore, much of the best skiing (for advanced or expert skiers) requires finding obscure traverses or some hiking. The only solution is simply to stick with it. One day—one run, even—will be your epiphany, and suddenly Alta will explode upon you with possibilities. Albion Basin's lower slopes have a terrific expanse of novice and lower-intermediate terrain. Rolling meadows combine as perhaps the best place in the country for lesser-skilled skiers to learn to ski powder. Two-hour lessons start at $30. Half-day group lessons for adults and children are available. Box 8007, 84092, tel. 801/359–1078, 888/

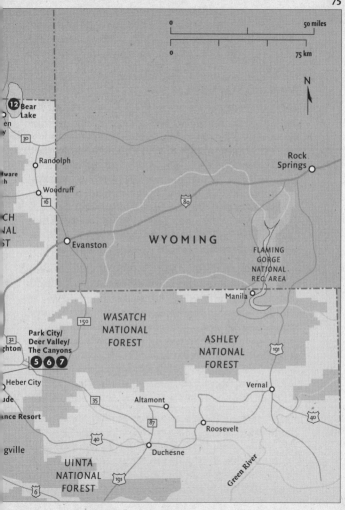

782–9258 central lodging reservations, 801/572–3939 snow report, www.alta.com or www.altaskiarea.com. 2,100-ft vertical drop; 2,200 skiable acres; 25% novice, 40% intermediate, 35% advanced; 6 double chairs, 2 triple chairs. Lift tickets: $35.

Where to Stay and Eat

$$$$ **RUSTLER LODGE.** Alta's fanciest lodge resembles a traditional full-service hotel. The interior is decidedly upscale; common areas have dark wood paneling, burgundy chairs and couches, and handsome wooden backgammon tables. Guest quarters are warmly decorated with dark woods, white brick walls, and richly colored fabrics. Larger rooms have sofas and seating areas. All but three units have private baths. As at all of Alta's lodges, breakfast and dinner are included in the price. Box 8030, 84092, tel. 801/742–2200 or 888/532–2582, fax 801/742–3832, www.rustlerlodge.com. 85 rooms, 4 dorms. Restaurant, bar, lobby lounge, outdoor pool, indoor hot tub, 2 saunas, spa, ski shop, children's programs, coin laundry. No credit cards. MAP.

$$$–$$$$ **SHALLOW SHAFT.** For fine beef, seafood, poultry, and pasta dishes, Alta's only base-area sit-down restaurant that's not part of a hotel is the place to go. The small interior is cozy and decorated in funky southwestern style, with a sandy color scheme and walls adorned with 19th-century mining tools found on the mountain. The menu is also southwestern, with such adventurous specials as pork medallions braised in apple cider. The restaurant makes its own ice cream daily. Homemade pizza is also served, as is liquor. Across from Alta Lodge, tel. 801/742–2177. AE, D, MC, V.

$$–$$$$ **ALTA LODGE.** Built in 1939, this is the original lodge at Alta Ski Area. Wings were added later with wall-wide windows to afford excellent views. Although you won't find basic amenities such as a TV in your room (there's one in a common area), the lodge remains a good value for the money. Rte. 210, 84092, tel. 801/742–3500 or 800/707–2582, fax 801/742–3504, www.altalodge.com. 57 rooms, 7 share bath. Restaurant, bar, 2 hot tubs, sauna, cross-country skiing, downhill skiing, children's programs, coin laundry, business services. D, MC, V. MAP. Closed May–mid Nov.

$$–$$$ **ALTA PERUVIAN LODGE.** Après-ski means hot chocolate and
★ apple cider at this quintessential, rustic ski lodge. A large stone fireplace dominates the plant-filled lobby, and handcrafted blond-wood furniture and books invite you to relax after a day on the slopes. A picture window overlooks the outdoor pool and hot tub, with the mountain in the background. The family-style dining room and the bar upstairs are as cozy as the lobby. Guest rooms, some of them tiny and only half with private baths, range from simple dormitories to two-bedroom suites. Three meals a day at the in-house restaurant are included in the rate. Combine this with complimentary lift tickets and you have one-stop shopping— Alta style. Box 8017, 84092, tel. 801/742–3000 or 800/453–8488, fax 801/742–3007, www.altaperuvian.com. 65 rooms (30 with bath), 20 suites. Restaurant, bar, pool, outdoor hot tub, sauna, coin laundry, ski shop. AE, D, MC, V. FAP.

SNOWBIRD

❷ 1 mi from Alta via Rte. 210 west.

Since the early '70s, "the Bird" has taken skiing to new heights. It shares Little Cottonwood Canyon with Alta; unlike Alta, though, it's one of the nation's most modern ski facilities. Its fast tram quietly whisks skiers in stylish powder suits to the summit, and there are plenty of trail signs, most with Japanese translations.

Formed by the tireless path of an ancient glacier, Little Cottonwood Canyon cuts a swath through the Wasatch-Cache National Forest. Canyon walls are composed mostly of striated granite, and traditional climbing routes of varied difficulty abound. There are a few bolted routes as well. Down the canyon from Snowbird is the trailhead for the Red Pine Lake and White

Pine Lake trails. Some 3½ mi and 5 mi in, respectively, these mountain lakes make for great day hikes.

The Resort

An expert's dream and a novice's nightmare, **SNOWBIRD SKI AND SUMMER RESORT** has plenty of powder-filled chutes, bowls, and meadow areas. Like its neighbor, Alta, it's known for its expert runs: 45% of Snowbird is black-diamond terrain. In contrast, however, an extra $19 for a lift ticket will get you the speed, convenience, and impressive vertical drop (3,240 ft in one fell swoop) that only Snowbird's 125-passenger aerial tram can provide.

Its open bowls, such as Little Cloud and Regulator Johnson, are challenging; the Upper Cirque Chute and the Gad Chute are hair-raising. On deep-powder days—not uncommon at the Bird—these chutes are also exhilarating for skiers who like that sense of a cushioned free fall with every turn. If you're looking for intermediate cruising runs, there's the long, meandering Chips, a few runs from the Gad chairlifts. Of note is Snowbird's Mountain Experience Program, a combination of guidance and instruction for expert skiers in challenging, off-slope terrain and variable snow conditions. Full-day workshops for skiers of all levels start at $85, and 2½-hour lessons begin at $52.

At the base area, modern structures house guest rooms, restaurants, and nightclubs. The largest of these buildings, the Cliff Lodge, is like an entire ski village under one roof. The resort's special events department mounts a variety of entertainments throughout the year, including performances by the Utah Symphony, live jazz shows, food and wine festivals, and murder-mystery weekends. As a guest, you receive free membership to the Club at Snowbird and enjoy a drink at any of several base area lounges.

From Memorial Day weekend to October, Snowbird fires up its tram to ferry sightseers and hikers to the top. Off-road cyclists are discovering that the slopes make for some excellent, if strenuous, riding. The resort also has a competition-class outdoor climbing wall that's open to the public. *Box 929000, 9000 Little Cottonwood Canyon Rd., Snowbird 84092, tel. 801/742–2222, 801/521–6040, or 800/385–2002; 800/232–9542 lodging reservations; 801/933–2110 special events; 801/933–2100 snow report, fax 801/947–8227, www.snowbird.com. 3,240-ft vertical drop; 2,500 skiable acres; 25% novice, 30% intermediate, 45% advanced; 125-passenger tram, 2 quad lifts, 7 double chairs. Lift tickets: $54 tram and chairs, $45 chairlift only.*

Where to Stay and Eat

$$$$ **CLIFF LODGE.** With bare concrete walls, the 10-story structure
★ initially looks bland, but the beauty of its design is that it blends in with the scenery. And every window has a wonderful view. This is one of the finest lodges in the Rocky Mountains, with a friendly, helpful staff to match. Rooms are decorated mainly in appropriate mountain colors and desert pastels. The Cliff Spa has a rooftop pool, massage rooms, hot tubs, and steam rooms. Camp Snowbird offers summer activities for children. The 10th-floor Aerie restaurant serves such sumptuous dishes as grilled free-range chicken with winter vegetable pastina or aged New York strip steak with cognac peppercorn sauce. There's an impressive wine list as well as a sushi bar. You'll find several other fine restaurants in nearby lodges. *9900 E. Little Cottonwood Canyon Rd., Snowbird Ski and Summer Resort, 84092, tel. 801/742–2222 or 800/453–3000, fax 801/947–8227, www.snowbird.com. 464 rooms, 47 suites. 4 restaurants, 6 bars, 2 pools, hair salon, 4 hot tubs, sauna, spa, health club, baby-sitting, children's programs (ages 3–12), coin laundry, dry cleaning, laundry service, convention center, meeting room. AE, D, DC, MC, V.*

$$–$$$$ **IRON BLOSAM LODGE.** This Snowbird condominium lodging has accommodations and amenities to suit any traveler's needs, including studios, bedrooms with lofts, and one-bedroom suites. Many have fireplaces and balconies. *Rte. 210, 84092, tel. 801/742–2222 or 800/453–3000, fax 801/933–2148, www.snowbird.com. 159* rooms, 125 kitchenettes. Restaurant, 2 pools, hot tub, 2 tennis courts, gym, steam room, children's programs, coin laundry, business services, airport shuttle. AE, D, DC, MC, V. Closed 1 week Nov., 1 week May.

$$–$$$$ **STEAK PIT.** Views and food take precedence over interior design here. The dining room is warm and unpretentious, with some wood paneling and an expanse of glass. The menu offers well-prepared steak, chicken, baked potatoes, and fish. *Snowbird Plaza Ctr., Rte. 210, tel. 801/742–2222. AE, D, DC, MC, V. No lunch.*

BRIGHTON

3 *25 mi from Snowbird via Rte. 210 north and Rte. 190 east; 30 mi from Salt Lake City via I–15 south, I–215 east, Rte. 210 south, and Rte. 190 east.*

North of Snowbird in Big Cottonwood Canyon is the small, locally treasured Brighton Ski Resort. It offers a perfect combination: all the fluffy powder of Alta and Snowbird and all the quiet charm many large resorts have left behind.

The Resort

BRIGHTON SKI RESORT is a great place for families. It was the first in Utah to offer a kids-ski-free program, and it has received many awards for its service to children and parents. If you're looking for excitement, over one-third of the runs are for advanced skiers, and lifts provide access to extensive backcountry areas for the real experts. Two-hour group lessons are $26

The emphasis on value extends to Brighton Lodge, which is quiet, comfortable, and so reasonably priced (keep in mind that children 10 and under stay free) that you might be able to stretch your ski weekend into a full week. Situated right on the slopes, the lodge has a tradition of friendliness. Rooms ($80–$150) have few frills but are still comfortable. *Star Route, Brighton 84121, tel. 801/532–4731 or 800/873–5512 to resort and for lodge reservations, 801/532–4731, 800/873–5512 snow report, fax 435/649–1787, www.skibrighton.com.* 1,745 vertical drop; 850 skiable acres; 21% beginner, 40% intermediate, 39% advanced/expert; 3 high-speed quad chairs, 1 triple chair, 3 double chairs. Lift tickets: $37.

SOLITUDE

4 3 mi from Brighton via Rte. 190 west; 27 mi from Salt Lake City via I–15 south, I–215 east, Rte. 210 south, and Rte. 190 east.

The history of mining and skiing in Utah often go hand in hand, and that's certainly true of Solitude Mountain Resort. The area was named by miners, who came to Big Cottonwood Canyon in the early 1900s in search of silver. In the 1950s a man who had made his fortune in mining elsewhere decided to retire in the Wasatch Mountains and take up skiing. He left a local resort in a huff one day when he was denied use of the bathrooms, which were reserved for lodging guests. In revenge, he built a rival resort. The result is Solitude, which has served skiers since 1957 and now rivals many resorts in the West.

The Resort

Downhill skiing (half-day group lessons cost a modest $40) and snowboarding are the main attractions at **SOLITUDE MOUNTAIN RESORT.** There are also miles of snowshoe and cross-country trails at the Nordic Center. For $10, adults can use the trails all day; for $40, they receive an all-day trail pass and a one-hour private lesson.

During the past decade, Solitude has grown into a village, with lodges, condominiums, a luxury hotel, and award-winning restaurants. The emphasis is on comfort and on the creation of memorable experiences. A perfect example is the yurt dinner: after a guided snowshoe or cross-country ski trek through the forest, you enjoy an elegant 5-course dinner at a Mongolian hut. *12000 Big Cottonwood Canyon, Solitude 84121, tel. 801/534–1400 or 800/748–4754, 801/536–5774 Nordic Center, 801/536–5777 snow report, fax 435/649–5276, www.skisolitude.com. 2,047 vertical drop;*

*1,200 skiable acres; 20% beginner, 50% intermediate, 30% advanced;
1 high-speed quad chair, 2 triple chairs, 4 double chairs. Lift tickets: $39.*

PARK CITY, DEER VALLEY, AND THE CANYONS

5 6 7   *33 mi from Salt Lake City via I–80 east (to Exit 145) and Rte. 224 south.*

Silver was discovered here in 1868, and in the years immediately following, Park City became a rip-roaring mining town without rival. In the process it earned the nickname Sin City. Certainly it was uncommon for any town within spitting distance of Salt Lake to have more than two dozen saloons and a thriving red-light district. Despite the generosity of the mountains, Park City eventually fell victim to depressed silver prices. It wasn't until 1946 that its current livelihood began to take shape in the form of the small Snow Park ski hill, which opened a few miles south.

In 1963, Treasure Mountain Resort began operations with its skier's subway—an underground train and hoist system that ferried skiers to the mountain's top via old mining tunnels. Facilities were upgraded over time, and Treasure Mountain became the Park City Mountain Resort. Although it has a mind-numbing collection of condominiums, at Park City's heart is a historic downtown district that rings with authenticity and reminds you that this is a real town with real roots.

Most visitors come to here to ski, but Park City also serves as an excellent base camp for summer activities. Hiking trails are plentiful. A scenic drive over Guardsman Pass (via a gravel road that's passable for most vehicles) provides incredible mountain vistas. There are some acclaimed golf greens, hot-air ballooning is available, and mountain bikers find the ski slopes truly exceptional pedaling. With so much to offer both summer and winter visitors, the town now has three resorts, each with its own special qualities. The emphasis at the original Park City Mountain Resort is on skiing and socializing in town.

In a somewhat secluded area on the edge of Park City you can revel in the peace and creature comforts of Deer Valley. The Canyons is a rapidly growing destination resort just north of town; it ranks in the top five resorts in America in terms of overall ski area, and it combines luxury with a casual atmosphere. A free shuttle-bus system serves the town of Park City, the three resorts, and the many surrounding hotels. Although the shuttle is efficient, the region is fairly spread out, so a car can be helpful. Be sure to look into the Silver Passport, which starts at $58 per day and allows you to use the lifts at all three resorts.

The Resorts

With 100 trails and 3,300 acres of skiable terrain, including 650 acres of open bowls, the **PARK CITY MOUNTAIN RESORT** is one of Utah's largest complexes. Roughly half the terrain is rated as intermediate, but the slopes that line Jupiter Peak are revered by experts. The east face of Jupiter has some particularly hairy, rock-lined chutes. Portuguese Gap is an elevator shaft lined by trees, and a "six-pack" (six-passenger) chair in McConkey's Bowl provides access to additional steeps. Snowmaking covers 475 acres, and night skiers will delight in Pay Day, the longest lighted run in the Rockies.

Park City's main drawback is lack of length. Despite a vertical drop of 3,100 ft, it's hard putting together a run of more than about 1,400 vertical ft. The area is laid out as a series of segments rather than a single unit. That said, Park City probably has the best overall terrain mix of any area in Utah—enough to keep skiers of all abilities happy for days. Two-hour adult group lessons starts at $48. The popular snowboarding lessons are similarly priced. Children's programs are available and there are also excellent programs for skiers with disabilities and senior citizens. *Box 39, Northstar Dr., 84060, tel. 435/649–8111 or 800/ 222–7275; 800/222–7275 central lodging reservations; 435/647– 5449 or 800/222–7275 snow reports, fax 435/647–5374, www. parkcitymountain.com. 3,100-ft vertical drop; 3,300 skiable acres; 18%*

beginner, 43% intermediate, 39% advanced; 4 high-speed 6-passenger chairs, 1 high-speed quad chair, 5 triple chairs, 4 double chairs. Lift tickets: $60.

Two miles south of Park City, **DEER VALLEY** broke new ground in the ski industry by providing such amenities as ski valets, on-slope phones, grooming fit for a king, and slope-side dining of the highest caliber. For such pampering, the resort has won rave reviews from virtually every ski and travel magazine. It also offers extreme terrain in Empire Canyon.

The moderate pitch of the terrain and the quality of the grooming leads to skiing's version of ballroom dancing. Part of the ski experience here includes a two- to three-hour midday interlude of feasting on the Silver Lake Lodge buffet and catching major rays on the snow-covered meadow in front of the lodge—an area known appropriately as McHenry's Beach. The ski experience, in other words, fits right in with the resort's overall image. After a while, however, a sense of sameness can set in, so it's nice having Park City Mountain Resort next door. Five-hour adult group lessons start at $65. Private lessons start at $72 an hour. Box 1525, Park City 84060, tel. 435/649–1000 or 800/424–3337; 800/558–3337 central lodging reservations; 435/649–2000 snow reports, fax 435/645–6538, www.deervalley.com. 3,000-ft vertical drop; 1,750 skiable acres; 15% beginner, 50% intermediate, 35% advanced; 1 high-speed gondola, 4 high-speed quad chairs, 2 quad chairs, 9 triple chairs, 2 double chairs. Lift tickets: $63.

With a vertical drop of 3,190 ft, **THE CANYONS** has similar mountain terrain to that of neighboring Park City, but intermediates will find somewhat longer cruising runs here. Above-tree-line bowls feed into some fine tree skiing for experts. The resort has 3,625 acres of skiable terrain and is building a year-round base. As the first Park City mountain to allow snowboarding, this resort is popular with younger crowds. The Perfect Turn program bills itself as a "coaching" program, rather than an instructional program, for skiers and snowboarders of all ages. One hour private clinics start at $57 per person and $90 for two. 4000 The Canyons Resort Dr., Park City 84098, tel. 435/649–5400, 435/615–8040, or 888/226–9667; 888/226–9667 central lodging reservations; 435/615–3308 snow reports, fax 435/649–7374, www.thecanyons.com. 3,190-ft vertical drop; 3,625 skiable acres; 14% beginner, 44% intermediate, 42% advanced; 1 8-passenger gondola, 4 high-speed quad chairs, 4 quad chairs, 1 triple chair, 1 double chair, 1 surface lift. Lift tickets: $59.

SKI EQUIPMENT RENTALS

Several shops in the Park City area rent equipment packages, some for as little as $10 a day.

Advance rental reservations are available from **BREEZE SKI RENTALS** (1284 Lowell, Park City, near Pay Day lift, tel. 435/649–2736 or 800/525–0314; 1415 Lowell, Park City, near ice rink, tel. 435/649–1902; 4343 N. Highway 224, The Canyons, tel. 435/655–7066, www.skirentals.com), which has two locations in Park City and one in the Canyons. Rates range from $12 to $43 a day.

JAN'S MOUNTAIN OUTFITTERS (1600 Park Ave., Park City, tel. 435/649–4949 or 800/745–1020) offers not only equipment packages ($18 a day, $28 for high-performance) but also clothing rentals starting at $27 a day.

UTAH SKI & GOLF (698 Park Ave., Park City, tel. 435/649–3020; 1255 Empire Ave., Park City, in the Sweetwater Condo, tel. 435/655–8367, www.utahskigolf.com) has two shops in Park City and two at Salt Lake International Airport. It offers downhill and cross-country equipment, snowshoes, and clothing. Rates for downhill ski equipment range from $10 to $30 a day; complete ski packages, which include equipment and clothing, are $35 a day.

Other Outdoor Activities and Sports

The **ALPINE SLIDE** (1345 Lowell Ave., Park City, tel. 435/649–8111 or 800/222–7275) is a big attraction during the summer at the Park City Mountain Resort. Children of all ages can fly down the curving track on an easy-to-control sled.

ROCKPORT STATE PARK (9040 N. Rte. 302, Peoa, 7 mi south of Wanship on Rte. 32, tel. 435/336–2241), northeast of Park City, is a great place for boating and fishing. Eight camping areas allow for developed or primitive camping.

BACKCOUNTRY AND TRACK SKIING

Those interested in unguided skiing can climb the Guardsman's Pass Road, which is between Deer Valley and Park City and is closed to traffic in winter. Strong intermediates and better can reserve a three-canyon tour with **SKI UTAH INTERCONNECT ADVENTURE TOUR** (tel. 801/534–1907).

The only tracks in the area are at the **WHITE PINE SKI TOURING CENTER,** between Park City and the Canyons. The 20 groomed km (12 mi) are on a flat golf course that's nothing special as far as scenery or terrain are concerned but is adequate for anyone seeking a quick aerobic workout. Lessons and rentals are available. Box 680068, Park City 84068, tel. 801/649–8710 or 801/649–8701. Trail fee: $12.

BOBSLEDDING AND SKI JUMPING

At the **UTAH WINTER SPORTS PARK** (3000 Bear Hollow Dr., Park City, tel. 435/658–4200)—site of the 2002 Olympic bobsled, luge, and ski-jumping events—you can take recreational ski-jumping lessons or bobsled rides on actual Olympic courses. The park also serves as a year-round training site for members of the U.S. Ski Team and other athletes. In summer, check out the freestyle ski jumpers who practice on a special jump with a splash pool at the bottom.

CYCLING

Several mountain bike trails are accessible from the Guardsman Pass Road in Park City. Both Deer Valley Ski Resort and the Park City Mountain Resort run lifts in the summer to facilitate fun descents by bike. The Canyons also has cycling trails on the

Alf Engen's Ski Dream

Skiers racing down the runs at one of Utah's many resorts or enjoying a tram or chairlift ride to the top of the Wasatch Mountains might want to consider how much they take for granted. In 1930, when Norwegian Alf Engen came to Utah to compete for the world ski-jumping title, skiers hiked to the top.

The eight-time ski-jumping champion liked Utah's mountains so much that he made his home here. He went on to scope out possible runs at what became the Alta ski resort. The Collins lift, the nation's second (the first was in Sun Valley, Idaho), was constructed at Alta in the late 1930s, and lift tickets cost just 75 cents a day. Alf also had a hand in designing Brighton and Snowbasin. His legacy lives on at Snowbasin, site of the 2002 Winter Olympics alpine downhill events.

Although Alf left competition at age 55, sharing his love for winter sports was a life-long passion. He trained soldiers for service in the Alps during World War II, coached the U.S. Olympic ski team in 1948, and spent five decades as an instructor at Alta's ski school. His enthusiasm for life and skiing infected everyone. One look at the smiling senior citizen inspired many skiers to keep in shape. When Alf died in 2001 at age 90, skiing had become a major industry in Utah with 14 resorts. Alta remains the most historic and the closest to his vision. Because of this vision, there's a ski museum named in his honor at the Utah Winter Sports Park.

—By Tom and Gayen Wharton

resort property. The Historic Union Pacific Rail Trail is a 28-mi trail popular with cyclists. It begins at Park City and follows I–80 to Echo Reservoir.

GOLF
The **PARK CITY MUNICIPAL GOLF COURSE** (1541 Thaynes Canyon Dr., tel. 435/615–5800) has 18 holes.

HOT-AIR BALLOONING
PARK CITY BALLOON ADVENTURES (tel. 435/645–8787 or 800/396–8787) offers half-hour and one-hour scenic flights daily, weather permitting. Fliers meet at a local hotel and are shuttled to the take-off site, which varies from day to day. A Continental breakfast is served during the flight, and a champagne or non-alcoholic toast is offered on touch-down. Reservations are required.

Where to Stay and Eat

$$$$ ALL SEASONS. These deluxe condominiums next to the Park City Golf Course have spectacular views of the mountain as well as whirlpool tubs, sleeper sofas, fireplaces, hardwood floors, state-of-the-art kitchens, and a good many other comforts. Condos vary in size and can be rented for long periods. *1585 Empire Ave., Park City 84060, tel. 435/649–5500 or 800/331–8652, fax 435/649–6647, www.silverkinghotel.com. 16 condos. In-room VCRs, pool, coin laundry. AE, D, MC, V.*

$$$$ CHIMAYO. Designed after the Chimayo mission in Mexico, this attractive restaurant has fawn-color stone walls, tiles, and wooden ceiling trusses. It offers innovative dishes like crab-stuffed grouper steamed in a banana leaf, avocado slaw, and seared elk burritos. The wine list is eclectic, with Spanish and South American varietals. *368 Main St., Park City, tel. 435/649–6222. AE, D, MC, V. Closed May.*

$$$$ EDELWEISS HAUS. About 200 yards from the Park City Mountain Resort lifts and a pleasant walk from historic Main Street, these

When you pack your
MCI Calling Card, it's like packing
your loved ones along too.

Your MCI Calling Card is the easy way to stay in touch when you travel. Use it to call to and from over 125 countries. Plus, every time you call, you can earn frequent flier miles. So wherever your travels take you, call home with your MCI Calling Card. It's even easy to get one. Just visit **www.mci.com/worldphone**.

EASY TO CALL WORLDWIDE

1. Just enter the WorldPhone® access number of the country you're calling from.

2. Enter or give the operator your MCI Calling Card number.

3. Enter or give the number you're calling.

Argentina	0-800-222-6249
Bermuda ÷	1-800-888-8000
Brazil	000-8012
United States	1-800-888-8000

÷ Limited availability.

EARN FREQUENT FLIER MILES

SEE THE WORLD IN FULL COLOR

Fodor's Exploring Guides bring all the great sights vividly to life with hundreds of photographs, fascinating historical background, and colorful anecdotes. Detailed maps and practical information keep you headed in the right direction.

Pair a Fodor's Exploring Guide with your trusted Fodor's Pocket Guide for a complete planning package.

Fodor's EXPLORING GUIDES

At bookstores everywhere.

condos are spacious and up to date. They vary in size, though all have fully equipped kitchens. *1482 Empire Ave., Park City 84060, tel. 435/649–9342, 800/438–3855, or 800/245–6417, fax 435/649–4049, www.pclodge.com. 54 condos. Pool, hot tub, sauna, coin laundry, business services. AE, D, MC, V.*

$$$$ SILVER QUEEN. In historic Old Town, this inn blends Old World elegance with modern convenience. Rooms are individually decorated with antique furnishings, brass beds, cushioned chairs, and richly colored rugs. They have full kitchens, whirlpool tubs, fireplaces, and washer/dryer units. Ski lockers are available. *632 Main St., Park City 84060, tel. 435/649–5986 or 800/447–6423, fax 435/649–3572. 12 rooms. D, MC, V.*

$$$$ STEIN ERIKSEN LODGE. This upscale lodge at mid-mountain
★ has many an amenity in its spacious rooms and suites. Everything is done in light colors with a lot of unstained woodwork and furniture. Some rooms have hot tubs, fireplaces, and VCRs. The Glitretind restaurant ($22–$34, reservations essential) is posh but not ostentatious, gracious but not overbearing. As you might imagine, service is exemplary, and the decor is impeccable, with wood trim, cranberry tablecloths, crystal glasses, hand-painted china, and fresh-cut flowers. Dishes are creative. How does pepper-crusted duck breast sound? Most desserts feature delicate sugar work. *7700 Stein Way, Deer Valley 84060, tel. 435/649–3700 or 800/453–1302, fax 435/649–5825, www.steinlodge.com. 81 rooms, 50 suites. 2 restaurants, bar, in-room data ports, room service, pool, hot tub, massage, gym, mountain bikes, downhill skiing, sleigh rides, snowmobiling, business services. AE, D, DC, MC, V. BP.*

$$$$ YARROW RESORT HOTEL & CONFERENCE CENTER. Easy access to all three Park City resorts and a nearby golf course are the principal attractions here. Some rooms have fireplaces. *1800 Park Ave., Park City 84060, tel. 435/649–7000 or 800/927–7694, fax 435/649–4819, www.yarrowresort.com. 173 rooms, 8 suites. Restaurant,* bar, room service, pool, hot tub, health club, coin laundry, business services. AE, D, DC, MC, V.

$$$–$$$$ **★ GRAPPA.** In the Old Town district, this restaurant specializes in ambience and northern Italian dishes. Heavy floor tiles, bricks, and timbers lend a rustic, warm, farmhouse feel. Tables on the wraparound balcony overlook those on the first floor. The menus, which change seasonally, offer appetizers such as homemade duck prosciutto with a summer pear and balsamic vinegar salad. Innovative entrées include pancetta-wrapped chicken fricassee filled with spinach and mushroom risotto. 151 Main St., Park City, tel. 435/645–0636. AE, D, MC, V.

$$$–$$$$ **LODGE AT MOUNTAIN VILLAGE.** Rooms are spacious, modern, and bright at this deluxe wood-and-stone villa at the base of the Park City lifts. You can ski in and ski out, too. The condos have fireplaces, kitchenettes, floor-to-ceiling windows, stucco walls, and luxurious carpets. 1415 Lowell Ave., Park City 84060, tel. 435/649–0800, 435/658–3383, or 800/824–5331, fax 435/645–9132, www.davidhollands.com. 145 condos. Indoor-outdoor pool, hot tub, sauna, steam room, coin laundry. AE, D, DC, MC, V.

$$$–$$$$ **MARRIOTT HOTEL.** As one of Park City's largest, this hotel offers a full array of amenities, including underground parking, which makes it the preferred hotel of athletes who participate in the annual World Cup competition. The motif is Western, and the decor includes artifacts from region's mining era. On the premises are a restaurant and an atrium area with a pool. It's an easy walk from here to downtown shops and restaurants. 1895 Sidewinder Dr. (Box 4439), Park City 84060, tel. 435/649–2900 or 800/234–9003, fax 435/649–4852, www.parkcityutah.com. 199 rooms. Restaurant, bar, coffee shop, indoor pool, hot tub, sauna, gym, bicycles, mountain bikes, ski shop, laundry services, convention center, meetings rooms. AE, D, DC, MC, V.

$$$–$$$$ **SHADOW RIDGE RESORT.** From here, just a few feet from the Park City Mountain Resort, you can amble to the slopes in less time than it takes to warm up your car. Accommodations range from single hotel rooms to two-bedroom condominium suites with full kitchens. All rooms have sturdy furnishings in the colors of a mountain summer. The staff here is friendly and experienced. 50 Shadow Ridge St. (Box 1820), Park City 84060, tel. 435/655–3315 or 800/451–3031, fax 435/649–5951, www.shadowridgepc.com. 150 units. Bar, pool, hot tub, sauna, coin laundry, laundry services, meeting rooms. AE, D, DC, MC, V.

$$$–$$$$ **SILVER KING HOTEL.** Minutes from the ski lifts, this modern, luxurious condominium hotel has an expansive atrium lobby with a fireplace, plush sofas, huge windows, and exposed beams. Units vary in size, from studio to three-bedroom, and are made cozy with handmade furniture, pastel colors, and woven rugs. 1485 Empire Ave., Park City 84060, tel. 435/649–5500 or 800/331–8652, fax 435/649–6647, www.silverkinghotel.com. 62 units. In-room VCRs, pool, coin laundry. AE, D, MC, V.

$$$–$$$$ **SNOW FLOWER.** A four-building wooden complex beside a hill, this place is known more for its ski-in/ski-out convenience, varied rooms, and comparatively affordable rates than for its design. Because each unit is individually owned, rooms vary considerably in furnishings and style. All the condos have kitchens, fireplaces, and whirlpool tubs. 401 Silver King Dr., Park City 84060, tel. 435/649–6400 or 800/852–3101, fax 435/649–6049, www.snowflowerparkcity.com. 142 condos. In-room data ports, in-room VCRs, 2 pools, coin laundry. AE, D, MC, V.

$$$–$$$$ **350 MAIN.** Known for its fresh oysters, mussels, and shellfish, as well as tuna and sea-bass specials, this Old Town restaurant has verdigris-toned furniture and a rust-tinted ceiling. It's warm and inviting after a day on the slopes. 350 Main St., Park City, tel. 435/649–3140. AE, D, MC, V.

$$–$$$$ **INN AT PROSPECTOR SQUARE.** This all-condo property has accommodations that range from studios to three bedrooms. Standard rooms, furnished in pastels, have a queen-size bed and sleeper sofa. The two-story inn has grocery stores nearby, and kitchen areas are stocked with equipment and spices. Some rooms have hot tubs. *2200 Sidewinder Dr., 84060, tel. 435/649–7100 or 800/453–3812 (except Utah), fax 435/649–8377, www.prospectorsquarelodging.com. 200 units. Kitchenettes (some), in-room data ports, pool, hot tub, business services. AE, D, DC, MC, V.*

$$–$$$$ **1904 IMPERIAL HOTEL.** Built in 1904 as a boarding house for miners, the hotel has been restored to a more upscale turn-of-the-20th-century Western Victorian style. Each room is named after a local mine and has its own unique decor. Period antiques, fluffy robes, and down comforters are features common to all guest quarters. *221 Main St. (Box 1628), Park City 84060, tel. 435/649–1904 or 800/669–8824, fax 435/645–7421, www.1904imperial.com. 8 rooms, 2 suites. Hot tub. AE, D, MC, V. BP.*

$$–$$$$ **OLD MINERS' LODGE.** Built in 1893, the lodge is one block off Main Street, with individually decorated rooms named for famous and infamous locals. The entrance to the Black Jack Murphy Room—which has a rustic Victorian style—looks like the portal to a mine. You can walk to the town lift, which serves the Park City Mountain Resort. *615 Woodside Ave. (Box 2639), Park City 84060, tel. 435/645–8068 or 800/648–8068, fax 435/645–7420, www.oldminerslodge.com. 9 rooms, 3 suites. Hot tub, business services. AE, D, DC, MC, V. BP.*

$$–$$$$ **RIVERHORSE CAFÉ.** The two upper-level warehouse rooms that make up this café resemble an ultramodern big-city supper club, with exposed beams, polished hardwood floors, black-and-white furnishings, and walls adorned with original art. For your meal, choose from ahi tuna, charred rack of lamb, or the signature macadamia-crusted Alaskan halibut. Don't miss out on the mashed potatoes—they're famous. *540 Main St., Park City, tel. 435/649–3536. Reservations essential. AE, D, MC, V.*

$$–$$$$ ★ **WASHINGTON SCHOOL INN.** A three-story, stone, 1880s schoolhouse, which closed in the mid-1930s, was carefully restored in the 1980s to accommodate this inn's guest rooms, kitchen, and common areas. The interior is designer-perfect, with high, vaulted ceilings, cherry wainscoting, and a stunning center staircase leading to the bell tower. The large rooms and suites have Victorian-era furnishings and such features as country-style wall coverings, handwoven area rugs, tile-and-stone flooring, claw-foot tubs, and, in some rooms, four-poster canopy beds. Breakfast is served buffet-style in the dining room. At the complimentary afternoon tea, drinks and appetizers are served. 543 Park Ave. (Box 536), Park City 84060, tel. 435/649–3800 or 800/824–1672, fax 435/649–3802, www.washingtonschoolinn.com. 12 rooms, 3 suites. Dining room, hot tub, sauna, gym, laundry room. AE, D, DC, MC, V. BP.

$$-$$$ **BEST WESTERN LANDMARK INN.** Out by the interstate, this property makes is convenient if you want to split your time between Park City and Salt Lake. The rooms are nicely furnished, Continental breakfast is included in the price, and there's a small on-site convenience store. 6560 N. Landmark Dr., Park City 84098, tel. 435/649–7300 or 800/548–8824, fax 435/649–1760, www.bestwestern.com. 106 rooms. Restaurant, indoor pool, hot tub, exercise room, coin laundry. AE, D, DC, MC, V. CP.

$$-$$$ **CLAIMJUMPER.** At the center of historic Old Town, this lively restaurant is pure Americana, from its hardwood floors, green drapes, and grand stone fireplace to its emphasis on steaks, prime rib, and burgers. All the beef is aged, and cooked to your request. 573 Main St., Park City, tel. 435/649–8051. AE, D, DC, MC, V. No lunch.

$$-$$$ **ZOOM.** Owned by Robert Redford, this "western chic" eatery's specialty is . . . drum roll, please . . . macaroni and cheese! Suffice it to say it's nothing like the stuff in the box. The menu offers other comfort foods, but always kicked up a notch. Locals favor the tri-tip steak served with grits disguised by garlic and Asiago cheese, or the beefed-up, but totally meatless, Portobello mushroom burger. Leave room for the chocolate mousse cake with raspberry sauce. 660 Main St., Park City, tel. 435/649–9108. AE, D, DC, MC, V.

$$ HOLIDAY INN EXPRESS. With fireplaces and log furniture, this new hotel near the highway manages to convey the feel of a rustic cabin. A free shuttle service gets you to and from the Park City area resorts in winter. Continental breakfast is included in the rates. *1501 W. Ute Blvd., Park City 84098, tel. 435/658–1600 or 888/870–4386, fax 435/658–1600, www.basshotels.com. 76 rooms. Indoor pool, hot tub, sauna. AE, D, DC, MC, V. CP.*

$–$$ CAFÉ TERIGO. This airy café serves several well-prepared pasta and seafood dishes using only fresh ingredients. Good picks include almond-encrusted salmon or smoked chicken with sun-dried tomatoes over fettuccine. An order of bread pudding or mud pie tops off a meal perfectly. *424 Main St., Park City, tel. 435/645–9555. AE, D, MC, V.*

$–$$ EATING ESTABLISHMENT. Near the top of Main Street, this local favorite is known for its keep-you-skiing-all-morning breakfasts and its barbecue dinner specials. Dine on the patio in summer; the glass roof, atrium, fireplaces, and plants make winter seem warm and bright. *317 Main St., Park City, tel. 435/649–8284. AE, D, MC, V.*

$–$$ MAIN STREET PIZZA & NOODLE. Huge windows, a bright dining area, good no-frills food, and reasonable prices make this a family favorite. The pizzas are made California style, and the pastas and calzones are filling. *530 Main St., Park City, tel. 435/645–8878. AE, D, DC, MC, V.*

$–$$ NACHO MAMMA'S. In Prospector Square, just a few minutes from Main Street, this local favorite features southwestern dishes that will test your taste buds' heat tolerance. The chiles rellenos, which come with chicken, beef, or shrimp, push the upper limits of spicy, while the beef *chipotle*, with its thinly sliced meat and tangy sauce, sates any carnivore's appetite. *1821 Sidewinder Dr., Park City, tel. 435/645–8226. AE, D, MC, V.*

$–$$ **TEXAS RED'S PIT BARBECUE AND CHILI PARLOR.** Tables are crowded together in a friendly way in the southwestern-style dining room of this downtown eatery. Try catfish fillets or barbecued anything—ribs, beef brisket, pork, turkey, or chicken. 440 Main St., Park City, tel. 435/649–7337. AE, D, DC, MC, V.

$ **BAJA CANTINA.** Western artifacts and ski memorabilia are everywhere, and a sign on the door reads IF YOU HAVE RESERVATIONS, YOU ARE IN THE WRONG PLACE. It's known for burritos with anything and everything from pork to snow crab and black tiger prawns. 1284 Empire Ave., Park City, tel. 435/649–2252. AE, D, DC MC, V. Closed Sun.

$ **BURGIE'S.** Burgers (12 different versions of them), grilled chicken, and New York steak are a few of the classic American favorites served at this eatery. Saturday is salsa night, with music and dancing in a hall above the restaurant. Upstairs you'll also find a large-screen TV and pool tables. 570 Main St., Park City, tel. 435/649–0011. Reservations not accepted. AE, D, MC, V.

$ **EL CHUBASCO.** For a quick and hearty meal of traditional Mexican food, this popular place is perfect. Favorites are shrimp fajitas, *posole* (a rich soup that combines pork and dried corn in a chili-laden tomato base), fish tacos, and warm empanadas. The low-key atmosphere is part of the charm. 1890 Bonanza Dr., Park City, tel. 435/645–9114. AE, D, DC, MC V.

$ **MAIN STREET DELI.** This basic deli serves well-made classics like Reubens and Philly cheese steaks. There are also interesting vegetarian combos, hearty omelettes, and homemade granolas. 525 Main St., Park City, tel. 435/649–1110. Reservations not accepted. D, MC, V.

$ **MORNING RAY CAFÉ & BAKERY.** An urbane crowd favors this café for its specialty breads, bagels, and pastries, as well as its substantial omelettes, pancakes, and quiches. Wooden chairs and tables and yellow-tone walls hung with local art make the space inviting. 268 Main St., Park City, tel. 435/649–5686. AE, MC, V. No dinner in summer.

$ MT. AIR CAFÉ. Outside the Main Street hub, this country diner with booths and an old-fashioned counter serves large portions of familiar dishes. Ground sirloin, country-fried steak, and fish-and-chips are favorites. Breakfasts are hearty, and the fresh strawberry pie is a good finish to any meal. *Rtes. 248 and 224E, Park City, tel. 435/649–9868. Reservations not accepted. AE, MC, V.*

Shopping

Within the colorful structures that line Park City's Main Street are a number of clothing boutiques, sporting-goods stores, and gift shops. A few miles north of Park City, next to I–80, are the **FACTORY STORES AT PARK CITY** (6699 N. Landmark Dr., tel. 435/645–7078 or 888/746–7333). Represented in this collection of 47 outlets are Nike, Brooks Brothers, Eddie Bauer, Guess, and Corning.

Nightlife and the Arts

Among Park City's livelier bars is **CICERO'S** (306 Main St., tel. 435/649–5044), which offers live music most evenings and also serves good Italian and American food.

The historic **EGYPTIAN THEATRE** (328 Main St., tel. 435/649–9371), in downtown Park City, stages many different plays by local groups and national touring companies. The **PARK CITY INTERNATIONAL CHAMBER MUSIC FESTIVAL** (tel. 435/649–5309) runs from early July through mid-August. Deer Valley Resort's outdoor **SUMMER CONCERT SERIES** (tel. 435/649–1000) includes everything from classical to country music. The **SUMMIT INSTITUTE** (tel. 435/649–2315) at Deer Valley puts on musical and dance events throughout the summer. Included are performances by the Ririe-Woodbury Dance Company, a String Chamber Music Festival, and several artist-in-residence programs.

OGDEN

8 *35 mi from Salt Lake City via I–15 north.*

With a population of more than 65,000, Ogden combines a small-town feel with the infrastructure of a larger city. Brigham Young directed the settlement of Ogden in 1850, where mountain man Miles Goodyear had built a stockade and trading post.

Despite its Mormon roots, Ogden changed radically with the arrival of the transcontinental railroad in 1869. It quickly became a major Western crossroads and received an influx of non-Mormons. During World War II there was a considerable military presence here. This continues today, thanks to the proximity of Hill Air Force Base. Ogden is also a college town; Weber State University is within the city limits.

On your way into town from the south are Hill Air Force Base and the **HILL AEROSPACE MUSEUM.** Among the many planes housed in this large hangar are the SR-71 Blackbird (a reconnaissance aircraft that made a transatlantic flight in less than two hours), a B-17 Flying Fortress, and a plane first flown in 1911. Hill Air Force Base, Exit 341 off I–15, tel. 801/777–6868, www.hill.af.mil/museum. Free. Daily 9–4:30.

Built in 1924, the impressive Spanish Revival **OGDEN UNION STATION** demonstrates the esteem that railroad travel once enjoyed. The station now houses some interesting museums: the Utah State Railroad Museum, the Browning-Kimball Car Museum, and the Browning Firearms Museum. 25th St. and Wall Ave., tel. 801/629–8444. $3 (combined ticket to museums). Mon.–Sat. 10–6, Sun. 11–3.

Set in an impressive Victorian mansion, the **ECCLES COMMUNITY ART CENTER** has a permanent collection with works by such contemporary artists as LeConte Stewart, Henri Mosher, Pilar Pobil, David Jackson, and Richard Van Wagoner.

Also featured are a sculpture garden and changing exhibits and monthly displays of works by emerging Utah artists. *2580 Jefferson Ave., tel. 801/392–6935. Free. Weekdays 9–5, Sat. 9–3.*

Highlighting a chapter in history that unfolded decades prior to the railroad era, **FT. BUENAVENTURA STATE PARK** is a 32-acre tract with replicas of the stockade and cabins that Miles Goodyear built in 1846. Guides in period costume interpret the ways of the early trappers. Camping and picnicking facilities are available. *2450 A Ave., tel. 801/621–4808. $4 per vehicle. June–Sept., daily 8–8; Oct.–May, daily 8–5.*

In downtown Ogden the **OGDEN RIVER PARKWAY** runs for 3 mi to the mouth of Ogden Canyon. This urban greenway is where many people fish, bike, stroll, run, and play tennis or baseball. What really distinguishes the Ogden River Parkway, however, are two parks found along the way. The **MTC Learning Park** has botanical gardens and pavilion facilities; the **George S. Eccles Dinosaur Park** charges a small fee to view dozens of life-size dinosaur replicas in one of the largest collections of its kind in the nation. *1544 E. Park Blvd., tel. 801/393–3466. Dinosaur Park: $3.50. Dinosaur Park hrs vary by season and according to the weather.*

With the Ogden River Parkway pointing the way, follow scenic Route 39 into Ogden Canyon. A few miles beyond the canyon mouth, the mountains open up to make room for **PINEVIEW RESERVOIR.** In summer this 2,000-acre lake is festooned with colorful sailboards and the graceful arcs of water-skiers. The fishing is good, and beaches, campgrounds, and marinas dot the shore. Anderson Cove, on the lake's southern end, is popular, as is Middle Inlet, on the eastern shore. In winter the canyon provides some great (and inexpensive) alternatives to the Salt Lake City ski scene, including Snowbasin and Powder Mountain.

WILLARD BAY STATE PARK, about 10,000 acres in size, is actually a freshwater arm of Great Salt Lake. Fed by canals in the spring, it's effectively protected from saltwater intrusion by dikes. Because it's fresh water, Willard Bay is a popular fishing, boating, and bird-watching area. Facilities include a marina, concession stands, and shady picnic spots. Bald and golden eagles are spotted frequently in tall trees along the park's Eagle Beach. *15 mi north of Ogden off I–15, tel. 435/734–9494. $6 per vehicle. Daily 6 AM–10 PM.*

Where to Stay and Eat

$$–$$$$ **GRAY CLIFF LODGE RESTAURANT.** Set in scenic Ogden Canyon, this local favorite features Utah trout, prime rib, lamb, and seafood. Small touches such as lace tablecloths and linen napkins and a wall of windows that offers views of mountains and forests create a quiet, romantic atmosphere. *508 Ogden Canyon, Ogden, tel. 801/392–6775. AE, D, DC, MC, V.*

$$–$$$ **HISTORIC BEN LOMOND HOTEL.** Listed on the National Register
★ of Historic Places, the hotel is one of Ogden's most prominent structures; it's worth a peek inside just to see the hand-painted ceiling tiles and chandeliers. All the elegant suites are furnished with cherry-wood furniture, refrigerators, data ports, and two TVs. Monthly rates are available and are remarkably reasonable, making this a great base from which to mount an extended exploration of northern Utah. An on-site club features live music, a Manager's Social is held in the lobby on weekday evenings, and a full breakfast is included in the rates. *2510 Washington Blvd., 84401, tel. 801/627–1900, fax 801/394–5342, www.benlomondhotel.com. 144 suites. Restaurant, bar, in-room data ports, refrigerators, gym, nightclub, laundry services, free parking. AE, D, DC, MC, V. BP.*

$–$$$ **ROOSTER'S.** On historic 25th Street, this brew pub offers excellent
★ food and libations brewed on site. Pizzas, prime rib, and daily seafood specials are popular, as is the spicy seafood jambalaya. Wash down your meal with a tall Golden Spike Ale, or any of the brewmaster's specials, which vary by season. Sunday brunch

here is a lazy pleasure. 253 25th St., tel. 801/627–6171. AE, D, DC, MC, V.

$$ OGDEN MARRIOTT. Ogden's largest lodging facility is downtown, close to government offices and corporate headquarters for the aerospace industry. It's also within walking distance of the Ogden City Mall. 247 24th St., 84401, tel. 801/627–1190 or 800/421–7599, fax 801/394–6312, www.ogdenmarriott.com. 288 rooms, 4 suites. Restaurant, indoor pool, hot tub, health club, coin laundry, business services. AE, D, DC, MC, V.

$–$$ BAVARIAN CHALET. European collectibles, white tablecloths, candlelight, and traditional German cuisine create a decisively Old World ambience. The menu includes favorites such as Wiener schnitzel and sauerbraten as well as a few up-dated surprises. A sampler plate, with smaller portions of at least three different dishes, is popular, as is the Black Forest cake. 4387 Harrison Blvd., tel. 801/479–7561. AE, D, MC, V.

$–$$ CAJUN SKILLET. It's not unusual to see alligator dishes accompanying the fresh fish specials chalked on the north wall of this lively spot. The creatures are occasionally flown in by air express from Baton Rouge, where the owner's brothers raise catfish, frogs, and turtles. Locals come for gumbo, hush puppies, sweet-potato pie, and Cajun-style breakfasts. 2550 Washington Blvd., tel. 801/393–7702. AE, MC, V. Closed Sun.

$–$$ MADDOX RANCH HOUSE. Down-home Western food—steak, chicken, bison—and portions big enough to satisfy a ranch hand make this place, 12 mi north of Ogden, plenty popular. Every dish is made from scratch—people drive here from surrounding states just for a piece of the fresh peach pie in season. The friendly service is a delight. 1900 S. U.S. 89, Perry, tel. 435/723–8545. AE, D, DC, MC, V.

$–$$ SNOWBERRY INN. Overlooking Pineview Reservoir in the Wasatch Mountains above Ogden, this cozy inn is everything a rural B&B

should be. The quiet environment and views enhance the experience, as do the rustic yet comfortable rooms. The vegetarian breakfast is complete and country good. The inn is near three ski areas. *1315 N. Highway 158 (Box 795), Eden 84310, tel. 801/745–2634. 5 rooms, 2 suites. Hot tub, coin laundry. AE, D, MC, V. BP.*

$ BEST WESTERN HIGH COUNTRY INN. A rustic Western motif and a friendly staff make this place seem cozy. Jeremiah's restaurant serves hearty, locally acclaimed American fare for breakfast, lunch, and dinner. The motel is off I–15 and is close to the George S. Eccles Dinosaur Park. *1335 W. 12th St., 84404, tel. 801/394–9474 or 800/594–8979, fax 801/392–6589, www.bestwestern.com. 111 rooms. Restaurant, refrigerators, pool, hot tub, gym, coin laundry. AE, D, DC, MC, V.*

$ DAYS INN. Many amenities, a location near restaurants and shopping, and modest rates are the distinguishing characteristics of this chain property. For a $10 deposit, little Fido or Fifi can stay with you. *3306 Washington Blvd., 84001, tel. 801/399–5671, fax 801/ 621–0321, www.daysinn.com. 109 rooms. In-room data ports, indoor pool, hot tub, health club, coin laundry, laundry service, business services. AE, D, DC, MC, V. CP.*

$ SHOOTING STAR SALOON. From the dollar bills pinned to the ceiling to the stuffed head of a 300-pound St. Bernard on the wall, there's something to look at in every corner of this tavern. The menu doesn't stray far from burgers—those served here are considered by many to be the best in the country—and beer, and you can't beat the frontier bar atmosphere. *7350 E. 200 South St., Huntsville, 17 mi from Ogden via Rte. 39, tel. 801/745–2002. No credit cards.*

Outdoor Activities and Sports

GOLF

The 18-hole **BEN LOMOND GOLF COURSE** (1800 N. Hwy. 89, Harrisville, tel. 801/782–7754) has a serene setting with Wasatch Mountain views. While playing 18 holes at the **MOUNT**

A Step Backward Is a Step Forward

Unlike its mostly Mormon neighbors, Ogden grew up as a railroad town and later a military community. The city's 25th Street once served as the area's red-light district. At one time it was so full of brothels, opium dens, and saloons that it came to be known as Two-Bit Street.

By stepping back in time, Ogden's city managers have moved forward. Today the buildings that once contained all the notorious businesses have been preserved and now house restaurants, clubs, and shops. You can dine at Rooster's, an upscale brewpub set in a 104-year-old building that was once a Chinese laundry. Wash your meal down with such specialty beers as Polygamy Pale Ale. Or head for the neon dragon of the Star Noodle restaurant, where the Chinese are still represented.

Jazz greats once stopped in Ogden because of the railroad. Today Beatniks, a private club, offers live jazz much of the week. Nearby are Brewskies sports bar as well as The Club, which is filled with Beatles memorabilia. An old-time barbershop shares its space with cowboy artifacts that are for sale. Lattè and pastries are served at an antique wooden counter in a coffee bar. Crafts boutiques, antiques shops, kitchen stores, and an old hotel or two add to the eclectic collection.

The old Union Pacific railroad station dominates the street's west end. Here you can see Ogden native John Browning's gun collection as well as antique cars and train memorabilia. There's also a train shop. Stop at the visitor's bureau inside the station to pick up souvenirs or the free 25th Street walking-tour brochure.

—By Tom and Gayen Wharton

OGDEN GOLF COURSE (3000 Taylor Ave., tel. 801/629–0699), try not to let the stunning view of Ogden Valley distract you. Just minutes from downtown Ogden, the 18 holes of the **RIVERSIDE GOLF COURSE** (460 S. Weber Dr., tel. 801/399–4636) wind along the scenic Ogden River.

RAFTING

For a white-water adventure the whole family can enjoy, try rafting the Weber River on a tour with **PARK CITY RAFTING** (1105 N. Taggert La., Morgan, tel. 435/655–3800). The relatively gentle two-hour trip is a great way to experience a rugged canyon, and there are several mild rapids (Class II–III) to provide excitement. All equipment is provided.

DOWNHILL SKIING

Rising north of Ogden Canyon's Pineview Reservoir is **POWDER MOUNTAIN** (Hwy. 158, Eden, tel. 801/745–3772). As the name suggests, it receives a generous helping of the white stuff for which Utah is famous. It offers just under 2,000 vertical ft, three chairlifts, and three surface tows. Skiable acreage totals 1,800, and two slope-side eateries provide après-ski diversions.

A vertical drop of 2,950 ft made **SNOWBASIN** (Hwy. 226, Huntsville, 17 mi from Ogden, tel. 801/399–1135) the perfect site for the downhill ski races during the 2002 Olympic Winter Games. With nine chairlifts accessing more than 3,000 acres of skiable terrain, this is one of Utah's largest resorts. Snowbasin has no base-area accommodations.

Nightlife and the Arts

CLUB ESQUIRE: HOUSE OF BLUES (2510 Washington Blvd., tel. 801/612–3060), in the Historic Ben Lomond Hotel, is a great place to relax and hear blues bands. The **PERRY EGYPTIAN THEATER** (2415 Washington Blvd., tel. 801/395–3200) is an art deco jewel where plays are staged and, occasionally, films are shown. **WEBER STATE UNIVERSITY** (3750 Harrison Blvd., tel.

801/626–6000) regularly offers theater, music, and dance performances by students and visiting artists at the Val A. Browning Center for the Performing Arts.

GOLDEN SPIKE NATIONAL HISTORIC SITE

9 *54 mi from Ogden via I–15 north (to Exit 368 at Brigham City), Rte. 83 west.*

The Union Pacific and Central Pacific railroads met here at Promontory Summit on May 10, 1869, completing the first transcontinental rail route. Under the auspices of the National Park Service, **GOLDEN SPIKE NATIONAL HISTORIC SITE** has a visitor center, an auto tour, some vintage locomotives on display, and several locomotives that are still running. Every May 10 (and on Saturdays and holidays in summer), a reenactment of the driving of the golden spike is held. The nearest hub is Brigham City (population 16,000), which is, for many Utahns, synonymous with the sweetest peaches known to mankind. If you happen to be passing through in late summer or early fall, U.S. 89/91 between Ogden and Brigham is Utah's fruitway, with many produce stands and peach, apple, cherry, plum, pear, and apricot orchards. Brigham also has some century-old buildings grand enough to be striking. *Rte. 83, 32 mi west of Brigham City, tel. 435/471–2209, www.nps.gov/gosp/home. $7 per vehicle. June–August, daily 8–4:30; Sept.–May, daily 8–6.*

OFF THE BEATEN PATH **BEAR RIVER MIGRATORY BIRD REFUGE** – Thirty-seven miles from Ogden via I–15 north (to Exit 366 at Brigham City) and Forest Street (which becomes Bird Refuge Road) west, this refuge was originally a series of freshwater lagoons ideally suited for waterfowl. In 1983, however, the 74,000-acre preserve was inundated by the rising Great Salt Lake. Ice floes destroyed all its facilities and only after a considerable amount of work was the U.S. Fish and Wildlife Service able to resurrect a 12-mi driving tour that follows various dikes. The habitat has been reclaimed, and the refuge once again hosts seasonal influxes of ducks, geese, and shorebirds. Plans for a new visitor center are in the works, along with a proposed expansion of the acreage. *Bird Refuge Rd., 16 mi west of Brigham City, tel. 435/723–5887. Free. Daily dawn to dusk.*

Where to Stay and Eat

\$\$ CRYSTAL INN. The spacious rooms of this two-story motel have comfortable sitting areas with desks as well as such conveniences as microwaves, refrigerators, and VCRs; some rooms have Jacuzzis. There are mountain views from the swimming pool. *480 Westland Dr., Brigham City 84302, tel. 435/723–0440 or 800/408–0440, fax 435/723–0446, www.crystalinns.com. 52 suites. In-room data ports, in-room VCRs, indoor pool, hot tub, coin laundry, business services, meeting rooms. AE, D, DC, MC, V. CP.*

\$–\$\$ HOWARD JOHNSON INN. You're not far from the I–15/U.S. 89 split, and within walking distance of restaurants and historic buildings. *1167 S. Main St., Brigham City 84307, tel. 435/723–8511, fax 435/723–0957, www.hojo.com. 43 rooms, 1 suite. Indoor pool, hot tub, business services. AE, D, DC, MC, V. CP.*

\$ GALAXIE MOTEL. Reasonable rates and some rooms with kitchen facilities attract students and senior citizens to this standard motel. *740 S. Main St., Brigham City 84302, tel. 435/723–3439 or 800/577–4315, fax 435/734–2049. 29 rooms. Kitchenettes (some). AE, D, DC, MC, V.*

\$ IDLE ISLE. Built in 1921, this café maintains its wooden booths and player piano, and the old menus feature home-style dishes like beef pot roast and halibut steak, with memorable desserts. *24 S. Main St., tel. 435/734–2468. AE, D, MC, V. Closed Sun.*

CACHE VALLEY

10 *18 mi from Brigham City via U.S. 89/91 north.*

East of Brigham City, U.S. 89/91 tops Sardine Summit in Wellsville Canyon before dropping into the highly scenic Cache Valley. Walled in on the west by the imposing Wellsville Mountains (often touted as the steepest incline of any range in the country) and on the east by the Bear River Range (a subrange of the Wasatch), Cache Valley is 15 mi wide and 60 mi long.

The valley was originally home to bands of Northwestern Shoshone. During the 1820s it became a favorite haunt for Jim Bridger and other mountain men who often stashed (or "cached") their furs and held rendezvous here. Mormon pioneers, led by Peter Maughan, arrived in 1856 and created permanent settlements. Today Cache Valley is one of Utah's most important agricultural regions. Topping the list of foods produced here is cheese. One of three cheese factories in the valley, Cache Valley Cheese is the nation's largest producer of Swiss cheese.

To learn about Cache Valley's history from 1820 to 1920, visit the **AMERICAN WEST HERITAGE CENTER,** which features a 1917 living-history farm, a pioneer site, and a Shoshone encampment. On the farm antique implements are on display, draft horses still pull their weight, workers dressed in period clothing demonstrate sheepshearing and quilting, and special events take place throughout the year. The Festival of the American West, held at the center in July, features additional displays and reenactments, along with food booths, cowboy poetry readings, and concerts. 4025 S. U.S. 89/91, Wellsville, tel. 435/245–6050 or 800/225–3378, www.americanwestcenter.org. $3–$5. Memorial Day–Labor Day, Mon.–Sat. 10–5.

Mountain Men

The men who once forged paths through the wilderness in search of beaver, otter, and other furry creatures aren't needed to supply the wants of 21st-century fashion. Waterproof jackets, hiking boots with lug soles, and nylon backpacks have long since replaced beaver-pelt hats, buckskins, and moccasins. But the spirit of men like Jedediah Smith, Jim Bridger, Miles Goodyear, and Peter Skene Ogden lives on in the hearts of many.

The fur-trading business attracted many colorful characters—often they were loners, always they were adventurers. Some lived and trapped in small groups. Others saw other humans only at mountain-men rendezvous to exchange goods and news. The Native Americans often taught these trappers how to survive, and many of the mountain men had Native American wives and families.

Today private organizations sponsor mountain-men rendezvous throughout Utah. Visitors watch participants in buckskins or furs work on Indian beadwork or stir up Dutch-oven meals. There are skilled gunsmiths, tanners, leatherworkers, and hat makers. The crack of black-powder muskets echoes in the distance while Indian drums lure everyone into a circle dance.

The men and women who attend these rendezvous do so as a brief escape from the modern world. They come to barter, share ideas, and exchange stories. And though there's dancing, the meetings are seldom as uproarious as in times past; after all, there are many more opportunities to party these days.

—By Tom and Gayen Wharton

LOGAN

11 25 mi from Brigham City via U.S. 89/91 north.

Logan is home to **UTAH STATE UNIVERSITY** (tel. 435/797–1000) a land-grant college established in 1888. Today USU has an enrollment of well over 20,000 and is a leader in such diverse fields as agriculture, natural resources, and space technology. Just east of downtown Logan, the USU campus is best toured by starting at the historic Old Main administration building—look for the bell tower.

Across campus, the Chase Fine Arts Center includes the **Nora Eccles Art Museum** (tel. 435/797–1414, free, weekdays 10:30–4:30), with exhibits of works by locally, nationally, and internationally recognized artists. No visit to USU would be complete without a stop at the **Food Science Building** (1200 East and 750 North Sts.) for a scoop of the university's famous ice cream. You can also get breakfast and a lunch or dinner of soup and sandwiches here.

The twin towers of Logan's **MORMON TEMPLE** (100 North and 200 East Sts.) remind all that this college town is also a conservative community with Mormon roots. Rising from a grassy knoll, this impressive limestone edifice took settlers seven years to complete. The site was chosen by Brigham Young in 1877, and the work was directed by architect Truman O. Angell, designer of the Salt Lake temple. As with all Mormon temples, it's open only to followers of the faith.

Historic **MAIN STREET** is best explored on a walking tour; an illustrated brochure, available from the **Chamber of Commerce** (160 N. Main St.), guides you along both sides and up a few cross streets. The more interesting buildings include the LDS Tabernacle (open to non-Mormons); St. John's Episcopal Church, representing Cache Valley's first non-Mormon denomination; the Ellen Eccles and Lyric theaters; and the Cache County Courthouse, with its restored cupola. Stop in at the **Bluebird** (19 N. Main St., tel. 435/752–3155) to admire the early 1900s decor and to enjoy hand-crafted chocolates, a cool drink, or an ice-cream treat at the soda fountain.

If you pass through in the winter, be sure to drive up Blacksmith Fork Canyon to the **HARDWARE RANCH.** Here the State Division of Wildlife Resources feeds several hundred head of elk through the snowy months. A 20-minute sleigh ride takes you up close to the majestic creatures; call ahead to combine your sleigh ride with an excellent barbecue dinner. There's also a visitor center and a café. *Rte. 101, 24 mi southeast of Logan via U.S. 165 and Rte. 101, Hyrum, tel. 435/753–6206; 435/753–6168 (sleigh ride and dinner reservations), www.hardwareranch.com. Sleigh rides: $6. Mid-Dec.–mid-Mar., daily 10–5, snow conditions permitting.*

OFF THE BEATEN PATH **LOGAN CANYON** – From Logan, U.S. 89 continues for 30 mi up Logan Canyon before topping out at the crest of the Bear River Range. Within the canyon are a number of campgrounds and picnic areas administered by the Wasatch–Cache National Forest. For a particularly satisfying excursion, drive the 7-mi side road (marked) to Tony Grove Lake. At more than 8,000 ft, this subalpine jewel is surrounded by cliffs and meadows filled in summer with a stunning profusion of wildflowers. A short trail circles the lake, and other backcountry routes enter the Mt. Naomi Wilderness Area to the west.

Where to Stay and Eat

$$–$$$$ **PROVIDENCE INN.** The stone part of the three-story stone and cream-brick inn was once the Old Rock Church, built in 1889. Such architectural embellishments as Palladian windows lend the structure considerable elegance. Rooms are individually decorated—some Colonial style, some Georgian, and some Victorian. *10 S. Main St., Providence 84332, tel. 435/752–3432 or 800/480–4943, fax 435/752–3482, www.providenceinn.com. 12 rooms, 3* *suites. Picnic area, in-room data ports, in-room VCRs, hot tubs, business services. AE, D, DC, MC, V. BP.*

$$–$$$ **ANNIVERSARY INN.** On a historic boulevard, this inn actually
★ consists of three buildings, including a 22-room mansion that dates
from the late 1800s and a carriage house. Guest rooms, called
fantasy suites, vary in size and decor. The Honeymoon Suite is
elaborately romantic, and the Jesse James Hideout and the Swiss
Family Robinson suites are true to their respective themes. All
rooms have two-person whirlpool tubs, and a Continental breakfast
is delivered to your door. *169 E. Center St., Logan 84321, tel. 435/752–
3443 or 800/574–7605, www.anniversaryinn.com. 21 rooms. AE, D,
MC, V. CP.*

$$ **LOGAN HOUSE INN.** Built in 1895, this bed-and-breakfast features
an interior furnished in keeping with the period. The grounds are
lovely, and the complimentary afternoon snacks are a kind touch.
*168 N. 100 East St., Logan 84321, tel. 435/752–7727 or 800/478–7459
(reservations), fax 435/752–0092, www.loganhouseinn.com. 6 rooms.
In-room data ports, in-room VCRs, hot tub, laundry service, business
services. AE, D, DC, MC, V. BP.*

$–$$ **BAUGH BEST WESTERN MOTEL.** Rooms here are basic, yet
comfortable; they're also among the best deals in town. Because
the place is locally owned, the service is personable enough to
make up for the generic motel-style furnishings. *153 S. Main St.,
Logan 84321, tel. 435/752–5220 or 800/462–4154, fax 435/752–
3251. 78 rooms. Restaurant, pool. AE, D, DC, MC, V.*

$–$$ **DAYS INN.** A quiet property between Logan's downtown and
verdant farmland to the south, the inn is 2 mi from a mall and 2
mi from Utah State University. The rooms were renovated in 2000,
and some have kitchenettes. *364 S. Main St., Logan 84321, tel. 435/
753–5623, fax 435/753–3357, www.daysinn.com. 64 rooms. Kitchenettes
(some), indoor pool, hot tub, coin laundry. AE, D, DC, MC, V. CP.*

$–$$ GIA'S ITALIAN RESTAURANT. Upstairs you enjoy sit-down service and carefully prepared Italian dishes. Downstairs, in the Factory, it's strictly cafeteria style—the food includes pizza and sandwiches, and the atmosphere is lively. As any college student will tell you, the basement is where you go to meet friends for a beer; upstairs is reserved for entertaining a date or your parents. 119 S. Main St., tel. 435/752–8384. AE, D, MC, V.

$ CALLAWAY'S. The cuisine here is what a fine chef from Italy might develop after visiting southern California and the Southwest. Ravioli, linguine, and fettucine are all prepared with a creative twist. Santa Fe Alfredo is a good example, as are the dishes that feature bison. Hot breadsticks and a dipping sauce are served with each meal; these and a bowl of delicately seasoned soup will satisfy diners with smaller appetites. For dessert, try the decadent chocolate cake. The food is definitely worth the 6-mi drive from Logan (north on U.S. 91). 54 N. Main St., Smithfield, tel. 435/563–9179. AE, MC, V.

$ TANPOPO. In a small shopping plaza, this family-run restaurant serves Japanese food that has both taste and visual appeal. Begin lunch or dinner with something from the sushi bar—dragon rolls are popular, along with the shrimp tempura and California rolls. Favorite entrées include salmon teriyaki and shrimp and vegetable tempura. For special occasions, reserve a private dining room, where seating and service follow the traditional Japanese style. 55 W. 1000 North St., tel. 435/750–7099. AE, D, MC, V.

$ UNIVERSITY INN. This well-maintained property on the edge of the USU campus (it's actually part of the university) offers basic, comfortable rooms. Suites have in-room data ports, desks, and comfortable arm chairs. 4300 Old Main Hill, 84322, tel. 435/797–0016, 800/231–5634, or 888/222–5562, fax 435/797–1580. www.usu.edu/~univinn. 60 rooms, 14 suites. Business services, meeting rooms. AE, D, DC, MC, V.

Outdoor Activities and Sports

HYRUM STATE PARK (405 W. 300 South St., in northwest corner of Hyrum, tel. 435/245–6866) has a 450-acre reservoir that draws boaters in summer and fall. Shady picnic areas, a peaceful rural setting, and great views of the Wellsville Mountains and the Bear River Range make this a popular spot for family gatherings. In winter, ice fishing is the activity of choice.

CANOEING

Although you can canoe on virtually any body of water in the region, the best places include Tony Grove Lake in Logan Canyon and Bear River, northwest of Logan. Winding in serpentine fashion through Cache Valley, Bear River has several nice stretches, including a particularly satisfying one that runs 11 mi between Amalga and Tremonton. You pass a blue heron rookery along the way, so this is a good float for bird-watchers.

CYCLING AND HIKING

Road cyclists pedal out to the long, flat country roads of scenic Cache Valley or venture up Logan and Blacksmith Fork canyons. Mountain bikers can spend an afternoon on the 9-mi round trip from Wood Camp, in Logan Canyon, to the 3,200-year-old Jardine juniper tree that grows on a high ridge offering views of Wyoming and Idaho.

Mountain bikers and hikers alike can access a prime wilderness area via the 3-mi route from Tony Grove Lake to the summit of Naomi Peak. The Limber Pine Trail is a popular and easy hike (1 mi round-trip) at the summit between Logan Canyon and Bear Lake. In the Wellsville Mountains a 2-mi trail climbs steeply from Maple Bench to Stewart Pass, a lofty ridge along the migration route of eagles and hawks; on a clear day the view from here extends for more than 80 mi.

GOLF

The 18 holes of the **LOGAN RIVER MUNICIPAL GOLF COURSE** (1000 S. U.S. 89/91, Logan, tel. 435/750–0123) are surrounded by wetlands, shady groves of trees along the river, and wildlife viewing areas.

The Arts

Thanks to both the presence of the university and the community's keen interest in the arts, Logan offers many fine productions. USU's theater and music departments present a variety of exciting performances. The **ELLEN ECCLES THEATRE** (43 S. Main St., tel. 435/752–0026) presents Broadway musicals, Celtic music, and a yearly series of performances appropriate for children. The **LYRIC THEATRE** (28 W. Center St., tel. 435/797–0305) features plays by the university's repertory company. The **UTAH FESTIVAL OPERA COMPANY** (tel. 435/750–0300 or 800/262–0074) performs a 5-week season between July and August at the Ellen Eccles Theater.

BEAR LAKE

⑫ *41 mi from Logan (to Garden City) via U.S. 89 north.*

Eight miles wide and 20 mi long, Bear Lake is an unusual shade of blue, thanks to tiny bits of limestone in the water. It's home to five species of fish found nowhere else, including the Bonneville cisco, which draws fishermen during spawning in January. Among the lake's more discreet inhabitants is the Bear Lake Monster, which according to local lore lurks somewhere in the depths like its Loch Ness counterpart.

The Bear Lake area's signature cuisine centers around raspberries, which thrive in this mountain valley. Their abundance is celebrated during Bear Lake Raspberry Days, held each year at the beginning of August. Throughout the summer, several fast-food stands offer huge fresh raspberry shakes. You'll find several hotel and restaurant options in Garden City, which sits at the junction of U.S. 89 and Rte. 30, on Bear Lake. Most of the permanent residents here are farmers who wait out the cold winters just as farmers do everywhere.

BEAR LAKE STATE PARK–MARINA (U.S. 89, 2 mi north of Garden City, tel. 435/946–3343 or 800/322–3770) contains a marina, beach, picnic area, campground, and visitor center with information on all area parks. At **EASTSIDE STATE PARK** (10 mi north of Laketown), the lake bottom drops off quickly, making this a favorite spot among anglers and scuba divers. Facilities include a primitive campground and a boat ramp. **RENDEZVOUS BEACH STATE PARK** (Rte. 30, near Laketown) is on the south shore of Bear Lake and has more than a mile of sandy beaches, three campgrounds, and picnic areas. Taking its name from the mountain-man gatherings that took place here in 1827 and 1828, Rendezvous Beach hosts a reenactment of these events each September.

Where to Stay and Eat

$$$$ IDEAL BEACH RESORT. At this family resort on the shore of Bear Lake you can swim and boat, as well as play tennis and miniature golf. *2176 S. Bear Lake Blvd., Garden City 84028, tel. 435/946–3364 or 800/634–1018, fax 435/946–8519, www.ibeach.net. 36 condos. Restaurant, 2 pools, hot tub, 2 saunas, miniature golf, 6 tennis courts, business services. AE, DC, MC, V.*

$$–$$$ HARBOR VILLAGE RESORT. This resort has direct access to 300 mi of snowmobile trails (many area businesses rent vehicles). The condos vary in size and are pleasantly furnished. Guests mingle with locals and campers at Harbor Village's restaurant ($–$$$), one of the few restaurants in town that stays open year-round. It's a comfortable eatery that serves basic, well-made steak, seafood, and sandwich platters. *900 N. Bear Lake Blvd. (Box 201), Garden City 84028, tel. 435/946–3448, fax 435/946–2819, www.harborvillagerealty.com. 40 condos. Restaurant, indoor and outdoor pools, hot tub, sauna, gym. AE, D, DC, MC, V.*

$ LEBEAU'S DRIVE-IN. Although, there's no drive-up window, there's no microwave cuisine either—just old-fashioned fast food. The classic order would be a raspberry shake and a burger topped with ham, cheese, onions, and the homemade sauce. 69 N. Bear Lake Blvd., Garden City, tel. 435/946–8821. Reservations not accepted. MC, V. Closed Sun. and winter.

Outdoor Activities and Sports

CYCLING

In addition to the mountain-bike trails minutes away in Logan Canyon, a 48-mi loop trail circles Bear Lake. Cyclists of all abilities can enjoy all or any portion of this fairly level ride. The paved Lakeside Bicycle Path curves from Bear Lake Marina south and east along the shore, with several rest stops. Interpretive signs contain stories about Bear Lake's history and local lore.

GOLF

BEAR LAKE GOLF COURSE (Garden City, tel. 435/946–8742) offers nine holes in a charming, lake-side setting.

TIMPANOGOS CAVE NATIONAL MONUMENT

13 *36 mi from Salt Lake City via I–15 south and Rte. 92 east.*

Soaring 11,750-ft Mt. Timpanogos is the centerpiece of a wilderness area of the same name and towers over Timpanogos Cave National Monument, along Route 92 within American Fork Canyon. After a strenuous hike up a 1½-mi trail to the entrance, you can explore three caves connected by two manmade tunnels. Stalactites, stalagmites, and other formations make the 3-hour round-trip hike and tour worth the effort. No refreshments are available on the trail or at the cave, and the cave temperature is 45°F throughout the year, so bring water and warm clothes. Although there's some lighting inside the caves, a flashlight will make your explorations more interesting; it will also come in handy should you have to head back down the trail at dusk. These popular tours are often sold out; to guarantee your place, purchase tickets in advance. *Rte. 92, 3 mi from American Fork, tel. 801/756–5239 (cave information); 801/756–*

5238 (advance tickets), www.nps.gov/tica. Tours: $6. Early May–Oct., daily 7–5:30.

OFF THE
BEATEN
PATH
ALPINE LOOP SCENIC BYWAY – Beyond Timpanogos Cave, Route 92 continues up American Fork Canyon before branching off to climb behind Mt. Timpanogos itself. Designated the Alpine Loop Scenic Byway, this twisting road reveals some stunning scenery before dropping into Provo Canyon to the south. The 9-mi Timpooneke Trail and the 8-mi Aspen Trail, both off the byway, reach the summit of Mt. Timpanogos. Closed in winter, the Alpine Loop isn't recommended for motor homes and trucks pulling trailers. This is the roundabout way to get to scenic Provo Canyon from I–15; the more direct route is U.S. 189 east from Orem.

SUNDANCE RESORT

14 *51 mi from Salt Lake City via I–15 south and Rte. 52 east.*

The small but distinctive Sundance Resort, best accessed from Provo Canyon, came into being when Robert Redford purchased a ski hill in 1969. Reflecting the actor's interests in the environment and outdoor recreation, the resort was designed to blend in with its surroundings. In summer, hiking and biking trails and theater productions entice visitors. In winter the yearly Sundance Film Festival draws a wide audience. The festival has become an internationally recognized showcase for important films produced outside the mainstream studio system.

Where to Stay and Eat

$$$$
★
SUNDANCE COTTAGES. Ranging in size from one- to three-bedroom, these self-sufficient cottages have an appealing forest setting. All rooms feature natural-wood trim and handmade furniture; suites have rock fireplaces, decks, and kitchenettes. Whirlpool tubs are available in some accommodations. A spa offers herbal wraps, facials, massages, exercise equipment, and

an aerobics workout area, among other things. R.R. 3, Box A-1, 84604, tel. 801/225–4107 or 800/892–1600, fax 801/226–1937, www. sundanceresort.com. 20 rooms, 77 suites. Restaurant, bar, in-room VCRs, kitchenettes, massage, spa, aerobics, laundry service. AE, D, DC, MC, V.

$$$–$$$$ **TREE ROOM.** In addition to serving up great Continental cuisine
★ such as black bass with morels in a truffle sauce, this restaurant has a special ambience. The place is filled with exquisite Native American art and Western memorabilia collected by Robert Redford. The man does have good taste. Sundance Resort, R.R. 3, tel. 801/223–4200. AE, D, DC, MC, V.

$$–$$$ **FOUNDRY GRILL.** Wood-oven-baked pizzas, double-cut pork
★ chops with mashed potatoes, and spit-roasted chicken are among the hearty staples served up at this full-service restaurant. The view of alplike Mt. Timpanogos isn't bad, either. Sundance Resort, R.R. 3, tel. 801/223–4220. AE, D, DC, MC, V.

Shopping

The **GENERAL STORE** (Sundance Resort, R.R. 3, tel. 801/225–4107) is home base for the award-winning Sundance catalog and features distinctive home furnishings, clothing, and jewelry reflecting the Sundance ethic and style. Most practical for cozy evenings indoors is the good selection of beer, wine, and other spirits.

Outdoor Activities and Sports

Skiers at **SUNDANCE RESORT** (R.R. 3, Box A-1, off Rte. 52, tel. 801/225–4107 or 800/892–1600) will find 42 runs across 450 acres of terrain and four lifts that access the mountain's 2,150 vertical ft. In summer the mountain trails can be explored on bike or on foot.

Nightlife and the Arts

Nightlife at Sundance is low-key. Many guests opt to spend evenings relaxing in their cottages. The **OWL BAR** (tel. 801/225–

4107) has an ornate Western bar (bullet holes and all) that was originally in a Thermopolis, Wyoming, establishment frequented by the Hole in the Wall outlaws. There's live music nightly.

The summer **CHILDREN'S THEATRE** (Sundance Resort, tel. 801/225–4107 or 800/892–1600) features outdoor musicals for the little ones. In January the Sundance Institute presents the **SUNDANCE FILM FESTIVAL** (tel. 801/225–4107 or 800/892–1600), a renowned showcase for independent filmmakers with screenings and workshops at Sundance and in Salt Lake City, Ogden, and Park City. From mid-June through August the **SUNDANCE SUMMER THEATRE** stages Broadway musicals under the stars in a spectacular outdoor theater.

PROVO

15 *15 mi from Sundance via Rte. 52 west; 45 mi from Salt Lake City via I–15 south.*

Provo (population over 100,000) is one of the country's fastest-growing cities. With Mt. Timpanogos to the east and Utah Lake to the west, it's also one of the prettiest. The historic downtown section includes many small shops and family restaurants; the newer sections, stretching ever farther to the north and south of city center, contain malls, factory outlet stores, a variety of eateries, and the headquarters for several large corporations.

Provo and the entire region are probably best known as the home of **BRIGHAM YOUNG UNIVERSITY** (1230 North St. and Campus Dr.). The university was established by the Mormon church as the Brigham Young Academy in 1875, with a mandate to combine teaching about the sacred and the secular. It has grown into one of the world's largest church-affiliated universities, and it still reflects the conservative nature of the Mormon Church. Students must adhere to a strict dress and honor code and refrain from alcohol, tobacco, and caffeine. BYU is known for its large variety of undergraduate and graduate programs, is a considerable force in regional athletics, and serves as a cultural center for the southern Wasatch area. Heading up BYU attractions is a quartet of museums.

The collection of more than 14,000 works at the **MUSEUM OF ART AT BRIGHAM YOUNG UNIVERSITY** includes primarily American artists such as Maynard Dixon, Dorothea Lange, Albert Bierstadt, and Robert Henri, and emphasizes the Hudson River School and the American Impressionists. Utah artists are also represented with works from the Mormon pioneer era to the present. Rembrandt, Monet, and Rubens also turn up, along with some fine Far Eastern pieces. *N. Campus Dr., southeast of Cougar Stadium, tel. 801/378–2787, www.byu.edu/moa. Free. Mon. and Thurs. 10–9, Tues., Wed., and Fri. 10–6, Sat. noon–5.*

BYU's **MONTE L. BEAN LIFE SCIENCE MUSEUM** has exhibits on wildlife from around the world. The live reptile displays are captivating. *1430 North St., north of bell tower, tel. 801/378–5051. Free. Weekdays 10–9, Sat. 10–5.*

BYU's **EARTH SCIENCES MUSEUM** features dinosaur bones, fossils, and tours for adults and children. Kids love the hands-on activities, which include a table of artifacts they can touch. *1683 N. Canyon Rd., across from Cougar Stadium, tel. 801/378–3680. Free. Weekdays 9–5, Sat. noon–4.*

The **MUSEUM OF PEOPLES AND CULTURES** at BYU is an interesting student-curated collection of artifacts relating to cultures from all over the world. Works are housed in two galleries, and many exhibits focus on the peoples and cultures of the Americas. *700 N. 100 East St., tel. 801/378–6112. Free. Weekdays 9–5.*

In downtown Provo the **MCCURDY HISTORICAL DOLL MUSEUM** displays over 3,000 poppets from around the world in a private collection started by Laura McCurdy Clark. The facility also includes a doll hospital and a gift shop. *246 N. 100 East St., tel. 801/377–9935. $2. Tues.–Sat. noon–5.*

SEVEN PEAKS RESORT WATER PARK offers 26 acres of waterborne fun. When you splash down from a water slide or rope swing, there won't be a temperature shock since the water is heated. There are plenty of play areas and a wave pool as well. *1330 E. 300 North St., tel. 801/373–8777, www.sevenpeaks.com. $16.50. Memorial Day–Labor Day, Mon.–Sat. 11–8.*

OFF THE BEATEN PATH

SPRINGVILLE MUSEUM OF ART – Springville, 10 mi south of Provo on I–15 or U.S. 89, is known for its support of the arts, and its museum is a must stop for fine-arts fans. Beginning as a warehouse for works produced at the local high school, it later began to accept gifts from major artists. The present facility was built in 1937 and features mostly works by Utahns, among them Gary Lee Price, Richard Van Wagoner, and James T. Harwood. It also has a collection of Soviet working-class impressionism. *126 E. 400 South St., tel. 801/489–2727. Free. Tues., Thurs., Fri., and Sat. 10–5, Wed. 10–9, Sun. 3–6.*

HEBER VALLEY HISTORIC RAILROAD – In April of 1859, 11 men struggled through a snowslide in Provo Canyon to settle the verdant Heber Valley. Today this area, with several small towns, including Heber City (30 mi from Provo via U.S. 189 north and 20 mi from Park City via U.S. 40), still bears a resemblance to the farm valley of those settlers' dreams. The railroad tracks running along U.S. 189 are part of the scenic Heber Valley Historic Railroad. Following a line that first ran in 1899, trains take you on a nostalgic trip through beautiful Provo Canyon. Each car has been restored, and two of the engines—Number 618 and Number 1907—are fully operational, steam-powered locomotives. *450 S. 600 West St., Heber City, tel. 435/654–5601, www.hebervalleyrr.org. $12 and up. Daily 10–5.*

Where to Stay and Eat

$$–$$$ HINES MANSION BED & BREAKFAST. Much of the original woodwork, brick, and stained glass has been left intact at this 105-year-old mansion. Rooms are decorated around various themes and have period furniture, two-person Jacuzzis, and plenty of light. *383 W. 100 South St., 84601, tel. 801/374–8400 or 800/428–5636, fax 801/374–0823, www.hinesmansion.com. 9 rooms. In-room data ports. AE, D, DC, MC, V. BP.*

$$–$$$ MAGELBY'S. The fine meals are served in a building that's also an art gallery. Most of the artists represented—Gary Lee Price, Wolfe Barsch, and Bill Whitaker, among others—are nationally acclaimed Utahns. The steaks, seafood, and chicken are excellent, and the nearly three dozen homemade desserts are famous. *1675 N. 200 West St., tel. 801/374–6249. AE, D, MC, V. Closed Sun.*

$–$$$ RESTAURANT ROY. The freshly made pastas, meat dishes, and seafood can be accompanied by a wide variety of wines. Both the pepper steak and macadamia-encrusted halibut are popular. Classical music, an intimate atmosphere, and views of the Utah Valley and the Wasatch Mountains through French windows make this the place for a romantic meal. *2005 S. State St., Orem, tel. 801/235–9111. AE, D, DC, MC, V. Closed Sun. and Mon.*

$$ HOLIDAY INN. Proximity to U.S. 89 makes this a good place to stop. The rooms are comfortable and the amenities good. *1460 S. University Ave., 84601, tel. 801/374–9750, fax 801/377–1615, www.holiday-inn.com. 78 rooms. Restaurant, room service, pool, health club, business services. AE, D, DC, MC, V. CP.*

$$ PROVO MARRIOTT HOTEL. A large facility, this hotel close to downtown offers good service. Rooms and common areas have more sophisticated furnishings than many properties in this price range. And the Seasons Lounge, one of Provo's few private clubs, is a great place to go for drinks and music. *101 W. 100 North St., 84601, tel. 801/377–4700 or 800/777–7144, fax 801/377–4708,* www.marriott.com. 331 rooms. Restaurant, bar, indoor pool, outdoor pool, hot tub, sauna, gym. AE, D, DC, MC, V.

$–$$ BEST INN & SUITES. Next to the BYU campus, this chain inn is convenient to museums and shopping. Some pets are allowed for a $10 surcharge. 1555 N. Canyon Rd., 84604, tel. 801/374–6020, fax 801/374–0015, www.bestinn.com. 101 rooms, 4 suites. In-room data ports, indoor pool, hot tub, coin laundry, business services, meeting rooms. AE, D, DC, MC, V. CP.

$–$$ BEST WESTERN COTTONTREE INN. Close to BYU as well as downtown, this is a good choice for moderately priced lodging. There are indoor and outdoor pools, and you can get a pass to a nearby gym. A Continental breakfast is included in the rate. 2230 N. University Pkwy., 84604, tel. 801/373–7044, fax 801/375–5240. 80 rooms. In-room data ports, indoor pool, outdoor pool, laundry facilities. AE, D, DC, MC, V. CP.

$–$$ DAYS INN. Close to three major shopping areas, this chain property offers comfortable, contemporary rooms. Some pets are allowed. 1675 N. 200 West St., 84604, tel. 801/375–8600, fax 801/374–6654, www.daysinn.com. 49 rooms. In-room data ports, pool, business services. AE, D, DC, MC, V. CP.

$–$$ HOWARD JOHNSON. This is a good on-and-off stopover. It's easy to reach from I–15, but it's away from high-traffic areas. 1292 S. University Ave., 84601, tel. 801/374–2500, fax 801/373–1146, www.hojo.com. 115 rooms, 2 suites. Restaurant, pool, hot tub, gym, coin laundry, business services. AE, D, DC, MC, V. CP.

$–$$ PROVO COURTYARD BY MARRIOTT. As this hotel faces the Wasatch Range near BYU, some of its rooms have mountain views. Friendly service, comfortable common areas, and touches like fresh fruit and warm cookies in the evening give this chain a personal feel. 1600 N. Freedom Blvd., 84604, tel. 801/373–2222, fax 801/374–2207, www.provoctyd.com. 94 rooms, 6 suites. Restaurant, in-room data ports, room service, indoor pool, hot tub, gym, business services, meeting rooms. *AE, D, DC, MC, V.*

$ GANDOLFO'S DELICATESSEN. In a basement location, just odd enough to be interesting, you get a good variety of thick sandwiches, all named after New York City spots. *18 N. University St., tel. 801/375–3354. MC, V. Closed Sun.*

$ HOTEL ROBERTS. Basic, eclectic rooms for incredibly low prices characterize this historic hotel built in 1883 and remodeled in the 1920s. The lobby has a lot of woodwork, and some lovely old dressers and mirrors in the rooms date from the early 1900s. Not all rooms have private baths or TVs, so ask ahead about your accommodations. *192 S. University Ave., 84601, tel. 801/373–3400. 56 rooms. MC, V.*

$ OSAKA. An interior with clean lines, Japanese calligraphy on the walls, and the gentle light of lanterns over each table make a fine setting for a meal. Specialties include sashimi, gyoza, katsu, and tempura dishes. *46 W. Center St., tel. 801/373–1060. Reservations not accepted. AE, D, MC, V. Closed Sun.*

Outdoor Activities and Sports

CYCLING

In the Provo area, road cyclists may make a 100-mi circumnavigation of Utah Lake or tackle U.S. 189 through Provo Canyon or the Alpine Loop Scenic Byway.

FISHING

Provo Canyon has reputation for great trout fishing, but many locals claim to know better places in Utah to fish, and they complain that the area's reputation has resulted in overfishing. Maybe they're right, but believers are out here year-round laying out lines. They're presumably pulling something out of the Provo River to make that immersion in cold water worthwhile. A heavily used canyon road parallels the river, and the location—

just a few miles from downtown—makes this the sort of place where businesspeople can pull on waders over suit trousers and make a few casts after work.

ONSTREAM OUTFITTERS: FLYFISHING CONSULTANTS (1151 E. 230 South St., Provo, 84606, tel. 801/371–0891 or 888/593–4900, www.flyfishingutah.com) offers equipment and fishing excursions on the Provo River; the staff does everything except buy you a fishing license. **PROVO RIVER OUTFITTERS FLYFISHING GUIDE SERVICE** (916 E. 1150 North St., Pleasant Grove, 84062, tel. 801/785–5260 or 888/776–8824, www.utahflyfishing.com) has years of experience and will tailor a trip to fit your level of ability.

GOLF

The 27 holes at **EAST BAY GOLF COURSE** (1860 S. East Bay Blvd., tel. 801/373–6262) near Utah Lake give golfers a chance to meander along ponds and wetlands and to spot birds. There's something for golfers and those who must wait for them at **THANKSGIVING POINT** (3003 N. Thanksgiving Way, Lehi, tel. 801/768–2300 or 888/672–6040). In addition to the 18-hole, championship, Johnny Miller course there are greenhouses, gardens, and a barnyard animal park. Two large gift shops sell home-decor items and jewelry. The North American Museum of Ancient Life—with its dinosaur exhibits and its IMAX theater—is nearby, and the grounds are a pleasant place for a picnic.

ICE SKATING

PEAKS ICE ARENA includes a double ice sheet, open throughout the year for figure skating, hockey, and parties. One rink was chosen to host hockey matches during the 2002 Winter Olympics. 100 N. Seven Peaks Blvd., tel. 801/370–0452, fax 801/373–8711, www.peaksarena.com. $4. Hours vary; call for current information.

ROCKCLIMBING AND MOUNTAINEERING

American Fork Canyon, 10 mi north of Provo in the Uinta National Forest, has northern Utah's best sport climbing, with dozens of fixed routes. The steep walls also offer face, slab, and crack climbs. The **WILDERNESS SCHOOL** (72 W. 500 North St., Orem, tel. 801/221–0398, www.highangletechnologies.com) offers classes and guided climbing trips to American Fork Canyon and other areas in central and southeastern Utah.

WATER SPORTS

DEER CREEK STATE PARK (11 mi northeast of Provo on U.S. 189, tel. 435/654–0171) is popular with anglers and boaters, and it offers a quieter alternative to Utah Lake.

JORDANELLE STATE PARK has two recreation areas on a large mountain reservoir. The Hailstone Area is 10 mi north of Heber City via U.S. 40, with tent and RV camping and day use areas. There are also boat ramps, a children's playground, a visitor center, and a marina store where water toys (wave runners, and the like) can be rented. To the east, across the reservoir on Route 32, the Rock Cliff facilities are near the Provo River. This is a quiet area known for excellent wildlife watching, particularly along a series of elevated boardwalks winding through the aspen forest. The 50 campsites here are all walk-ins. The Rock Cliff Nature Center provides interpretation of the area's natural history. Tel. 435/649–9540 Hailstone; 435/783–3030 Rock Cliff. $6 per vehicle. May–Sept., daily 6–10; Oct.–Apr., daily 8–5.

Around Point of the Mountain (a popular hang-gliding haven and site of the Utah State Prison), I–15 drops into Utah Valley, much of which is covered by Utah Lake. Although the state's largest freshwater lake is 11 mi wide and 24 mi long, it averages a scant 9 ft deep. Boating and fishing are popular, but the cloudy water makes swimming questionable. On the east shore, **UTAH LAKE STATE PARK** (4400 W. Center St., tel. 801/375–0731) is the best access point. In addition to three boat ramps, campgrounds, picnic areas, and a marina, the park has a wheelchair-accessible fishing area.

Distance Conversion Chart

Kilometers/Miles

To change kilometers (km) to miles (mi), multiply km by .621.
To change mi to km, multiply mi by 1.61.

km to mi	mi to km
1 = .62	1 = 1.6
2 = 1.2	2 = 3.2
3 = 1.9	3 = 4.8
4 = 2.5	4 = 6.4
5 = 3.1	5 = 8.1
6 = 3.7	6 = 9.7
7 = 4.3	7 = 11.3
8 = 5.0	8 = 12.9

Meters/Feet

To change meters (m) to feet (ft), multiply m by 3.28.
To change ft to m, multiply ft by .305.

m to ft	ft to m
1 = 3.3	1 = .30
2 = 6.6	2 = .61
3 = 9.8	3 = .92
4 = 13.1	4 = 1.2
5 = 16.4	5 = 1.5
6 = 19.7	6 = 1.8
7 = 23.0	7 = 2.1
8 = 26.2	8 = 2.4

Nightlife and the Arts

Although Provo isn't completely "dry," the standards of BYU are very evident in the city's dearth of nightlife options. Bands and DJs keep things hopping at **ATCHAFALAYA** (210 W. Center St., just off I–15 at the Center St. exit, tel. 801/373–9014). Between dances and turns and karaoke, sample some spicy Cajun food. The **SEASONS LOUNGE** (101 W. 100 North St., tel. 801/377–4700) in the Provo Marriott Hotel is a casual gathering spot. The music is generally soft, making this a good place for quiet conversation.

Because **BYU** (tel. 801/378–4636) has a considerable interest in the arts, Provo is a great place to catch a play, dance performance, or musical production. There are a dozen performing groups in all. Of special note are the BYU International Folk Dancers and Ballroom Dancers.

PRACTICAL INFORMATION

Air Travel

AIRPORT & TRANSFERS

All the major car-rental agencies have desks at Salt Lake International Airport, which is 7 mi northwest of downtown. From the airport, take I–80 east to North Temple Street, which will take you directly to the city center.

The Utah Transit Authority (UTA) runs buses between the airport and the city center. Most downtown hotels offer guests free shuttle service. Yellow Cab provides 24-hour service to all of the Salt Lake Valley; other reliable companies are Ute Cab and City Cab. The ride from the airport into town will cost about $15.

➤ AIRPORT INFORMATION: Salt Lake City International Airport (tel. 801/575–2400).

➤ TAXIS & SHUTTLES: City Cab Company (tel. 801/363–8400 or 801/363–5550). UTA (tel. 801/743–3882 or 888/743–3882). Ute Cab Company (tel. 801/359–7788). Yellow Cab (tel. 801/521–2100, 801/521–1862, or 800/826–4746).

BOOKING

When you book, **look for nonstop flights** and **remember that "direct" flights stop at least once.** Try to avoid connecting flights, which require a change of plane. For more booking tips and to check prices and make on-line flight reservations, log on to www.fodors.com.

CARRIERS

Salt Lake City is served by America West, American, Continental, Delta, Northwest, Southwest, TWA, and United.

➤ MAJOR AIRLINES: American (tel. 800/433–7300). Continental (tel. 800/525–0280). Delta (tel. 800/221–1212). Northwest (tel. 800/225–2525). TWA (tel. 800/221–2000). United (tel. 800/241–6522).

➤ **SMALLER AIRLINES: America West** (tel. 800/235–9292). **Southwest** (tel. 800/435–9792).

CHECK-IN & BOARDING

If you're traveling during snow season, **allow extra time for the drive** to the airport. Weather conditions can slow you down more than you may have predicted. If you'll be checking skis, arrive early for your flight.

Assuming that not everyone with a ticket will show up, airlines routinely overbook planes. When everyone does, airlines ask for volunteers to give up their seats. In return, these volunteers usually get a certificate for a free flight and are rebooked on the next flight out. If there are not enough volunteers, the airline must choose who will be denied boarding. The first to get bumped are passengers who checked in late and those flying on discounted tickets, so **get to the gate and check in as early as possible,** especially during peak periods.

Always **bring a government-issued photo I.D. to the airport;** even when it's not required, a passport is best.

CUTTING COSTS

The least expensive airfares to Utah must usually be purchased in advance and are non-refundable. It's smart to **call a number of airlines,** and when you are quoted a good price, **book it on the spot**—the same fare may not be available the next day. Always **check different routings** and look into using different airports. Travel agents, especially low-fare specialists (*see* Discounts & Deals, *below*), are helpful.

Consolidators are another good source. They buy tickets for scheduled international flights at reduced rates from the airlines, then sell them at prices that beat the best fare available directly from the airlines, usually without restrictions. Sometimes you can even get your money back if you need to return the ticket. Carefully read the fine print detailing penalties for changes and cancellations, and **confirm your consolidator reservation with the airline.**

▶ **CONSOLIDATORS: Cheap Tickets** (tel. 800/377–1000). **Discount Airline Ticket Service** (tel. 800/576–1600). **Unitravel** (tel. 800/325–2222). **Up & Away Travel** (tel. 212/889–2345). **World Travel Network** (tel. 800/409–6753).

ENJOYING THE FLIGHT

For more legroom, **request an emergency-aisle seat.** Don't sit in the row in front of the emergency aisle or in front of a bulkhead, where seats may not recline. If you have dietary concerns, **ask for special meals when booking.** These can be vegetarian, low-cholesterol, or kosher, for example. On long flights, try to maintain a normal routine to help fight jet lag. At night, **get some sleep.** By day, **eat light meals, drink water** (not alcohol), and **move around the cabin** to stretch your legs. For additional jet-lag tips, consult *Fodor's FYI: Travel Fit & Healthy* (available at bookstores everywhere).

FLYING TIMES

Salt Lake City is approximately 5 hours from New York, 4 hours from Chicago, and 3¾ hours from Los Angeles.

HOW TO COMPLAIN

If your baggage goes astray or your flight goes awry, complain right away. Most carriers require that you **file a claim immediately.**

▶ **AIRLINE COMPLAINTS: U.S. Department of Transportation Aviation Consumer Protection Division** (C-75, Room 4107, Washington, DC 20590, tel. 202/366–2220, www.dot.gov/ airconsumer). **Federal Aviation Administration Consumer Hotline** (tel. 800/322–7873).

Bus Travel

Greyhound Lines runs several buses each day to Salt Lake's terminal at 160 West South Temple Street. The company also serves many other Wasatch Front communities: Tremonton, Logan, Brigham City, Ogden, and Provo. The UTA has frequent service to all of Salt Lake Valley, Davis and Weber counties, and Utah Valley. Buses, with ski racks, also make several runs a day to ski areas in Little and Big Cottonwood canyons.

➤ **BUS INFORMATION: Greyhound Lines** (tel. 801/355–9579 or 800/231–2222). **UTA** (tel. 801/743–3882 or 888/743–3882).

Business Hours

Most retail stores are open from 9 AM or 9:30 AM until 6 PM or 7 PM daily in downtown locations and until 9 or 10 in suburban shopping malls and in resort towns during high seasons. Downtown stores sometimes stay open later Thursday night, and many shops close their doors on Sunday. Normal banking hours are weekdays 9–5; some branches are also open on Saturday morning. Museums are generally open weekdays and Saturday from 10 AM to 6 PM; some have shorter hours on Saturday and Sunday, and still others are closed Sunday and/or Monday.

Cameras & Photography

Photographers love Utah—and with good reason. The scenery is America's best, and every season offers a multitude of breathtaking images. When you're at Native American sites, be sure to ask if taking pictures is appropriate. The *Kodak Guide to Shooting Great Travel Pictures* (available at bookstores everywhere) is loaded with tips.

➤ **PHOTO HELP: Kodak Information Center** (tel. 800/242–2424).

EQUIPMENT PRECAUTIONS

Don't pack film and equipment in checked luggage, where it is much more susceptible to damage. X-ray machines used to view checked luggage are becoming much more powerful and therefore are much more likely to ruin your film. Always **keep film and tape out of the sun.** Carry an extra supply of batteries, and **be prepared to turn on your camera or camcorder** to prove to security personnel that the device is real. Always **ask for hand inspection of film**, which becomes clouded after repeated exposure to airport X-ray machines, and **keep videotapes away from metal detectors.**

Car Rental

Rates in major cities run about $35 a day and $175 a week for an economy car with air-conditioning, automatic transmission, and unlimited mileage. This doesn't include tax on car rentals, which is 13.6% in Salt Lake City.

➤ **MAJOR AGENCIES: Alamo** (tel. 800/327–9633; 020/8759–6200 in the U.K., www.alamo.com). **Avis** (tel. 800/331–1212; 800/879–2847 in Canada; 02/9353–9000 in Australia; 09/525–1982 in New Zealand; 0870/606–0100 in the U.K., www.avis.com). **Budget** (tel. 800/527–0700; 0870/156–5656 in the U.K., www.budget.com). **Dollar** (tel. 800/800–4000; 0124/622–0111 in the U.K.; 02/9223–1444 in Australia, www.dollar.com). **Hertz** (tel. 800/654–3131; 800/263–0600 in Canada; 020/8897–2072 in the U.K.; 02/9669–2444 in Australia; 09/256–8690 in New Zealand, www.hertz.com). **National Car Rental** (tel. 800/227–7368; 020/8680–4800 in the U.K., www.nationalcar.com).

CUTTING COSTS

To get the best deal, **book through a travel agent who will shop around.** Also **price local car-rental companies,** although the service and maintenance may not be as good as those of a major player. Remember to ask about required deposits, cancellation penalties, and drop-off charges if you're planning to pick up the car in one city and leave it in another. If you're traveling during a holiday period, also make sure that a confirmed reservation guarantees you a car.

INSURANCE

When driving a rented car you are generally responsible for any damage to or loss of the vehicle as well as for any property damage or personal injury that you may cause. Before you rent, see what coverage your personal auto-insurance policy and credit cards provide.

For about $15 to $20 per day, rental companies sell protection, known as a collision- or loss-damage waiver (CDW or LDW), that eliminates your liability for damage to the car.

In most states you don't need a CDW if you have personal auto insurance or other liability insurance. However, **make sure you have enough coverage to pay for the car.** If you do not have auto insurance or an umbrella policy that covers damage to third parties, purchasing liability insurance and a CDW or LDW is highly recommended.

REQUIREMENTS & RESTRICTIONS

You must be 25 and have a valid driver's license to rent a car; most companies also require a major credit card. You'll pay extra for child seats (about $3 per day), which are compulsory for children under five, and for additional drivers (about $2 per day). Non-U.S. residents will need a reservation voucher, a passport, a driver's license, and a travel policy that covers each driver, to pick up a car.

SURCHARGES

Before you pick up a car in one city and leave it in another, **ask about drop-off charges or one-way service fees,** which can be substantial. Note, too, that some rental agencies charge extra if you return the car before the time specified in your contract. To avoid a hefty refueling fee, **fill the tank just before you turn in the car,** but be aware that gas stations near the rental outlet may overcharge.

Car Travel

The reconstruction of I–15—the main thoroughfare along the Wasatch Mountains—was completed in 2001, so highway travel around Salt Lake is quick and easy. From I–80, take I–15 north to 600 South Street to reach the city center. Salt Lake City's streets are extra wide and typically not congested. Most are two-way. Although not far from Alta and Snowbird as the crow flies, Park City, and its three ski resorts, is best accessed by following I–80 east from Salt Lake through Parley's Canyon. U.S. 89 branches to the north and south, U.S. 189 runs up Provo Canyon, and Route 132 winds into Sanpete County.

GASOLINE

In urban areas, stations are plentiful, and most stay open late (some are open 24 hours). In big cities, prices are similar to those in the rest of the continental United States. In rural areas, stations are less frequent, and hours are more limited, particularly on Sunday. In rural and resort towns, expect gas prices to be considerably higher than in large cities.

ROAD CONDITIONS

In urban areas, **expect heavy traffic** weekdays between 6 and 10 AM and again between 4 and 7 PM. To encourage carpooling, some freeways have special lanes for so-called high-occupancy vehicles (HOV)—cars carrying more than one passenger.

Roads range from well-paved multilane blacktop routes to barely graveled backcountry trails. Along larger highways, roadside stops with rest rooms, fast-food restaurants, and sundries stores are well spaced. Scenic routes and lookout points are clearly marked, enabling you to slow down and pull over to take in the views. Deer, elk, and even bears may try to get to the other side of a road just as you come along, so **watch out for wildlife on the highways.**

➤ **ROAD CONDITION INFORMATION: Utah Road Condition Information** (tel. 801/964–6000 in Salt Lake City area or 800/492–2400 within Utah).

ROAD SAFETY

Before setting out on any trip, **make sure your gas tank is full.** In rural areas, distances between gas stations can be great, making running in the reserve zone risky. **Be sure that your**

vehicle is in top condition. It's best to have a complete tune-up. At the very least, check the headlights and the brake, backup, and emergency lights; the tires, including the spare; the oil; the engine coolant; the windshield-washer fluid; the wiper blades; and the brakes. **Carry an emergency kit** containing flares or reflector triangles, jumper cables, an empty gas can, a fire extinguisher, a flashlight, a plastic tarp, blankets or a sleeping bag, warm clothes, food and water, and coins or calling card for phone calls (cell phones don't always work in high mountain areas). **Be prepared for winter driving conditions.** Note that winter weather isn't confined to winter months in the high country, so be prepared year-round. Tire chains, studs, or snow tires are essential. **Check the weather forecast and road conditions** before driving into high elevations. State police, tow trucks, and snow plows patrol major highways and lend assistance. If your car breaks down on an interstate, pull onto the shoulder and wait for help, or have your passengers wait while you walk to an emergency phone. If you carry a cell phone, try dialing *55, noting your location on the small green roadside mileage markers. **Don't leave your car if you become stranded in a snow storm.** Instead, wait—running the engine only if needed—until someone comes along.

RULES OF THE ROAD

Driving in the United States is on the right. Drive defensively and follow the posted speed limits. On major highways, the speed limit is 55 mph in urban areas; it increases to 65 or 75 mph on interstate highways in rural areas. But watch out. "Rural areas" are determined by census boundaries and sometimes make little sense. Increased speeds are allowed only where clearly posted. Transition zones from one speed limit to the next are indicated with pavement markings and signs. Fines are doubled for speeding in work zones and school zones.

Utah law requires seatbelts for drivers, front-seat passengers, and children under 10. Always **strap children under age 2 into**

approved child-safety seats. Helmets are required for motorcyclists and passengers under the age of 18.

Generally, right turns are allowed on a red light after the vehicle has come to a complete stop. Right turns on red are prohibited in some areas, but these are signed accordingly.

Children in Utah

Utah is tailor-made for family vacations, offering historic railroads, mining towns, the extreme natural features of national parks, wildlife, and many other outdoor activities. Visitor centers and local hotels/motels are often good at recommending places to spend time with children. Attractions often offer reduced family admission tickets.

Some trip organizers arrange backpacking outings specifically geared toward families with small children. Short half-day or full-day bike trips with plenty of flat riding are possible at resorts such as Park City. **Ask staff at local bike shops to recommended rides for children.** Be conservative in choosing a ride, though: altitude can be even more taxing on small lungs than it is on adult ones.

Fishing can be difficult, as the nuances of the sport and the patience it requires are often lost on children. **For family fishing trips visit lakes and reservoirs** rather than streams and rivers, because kids who are bored by fishing can go swimming, boating, or simply explore the shoreline. **Don't take children under seven on extended rafting trips** unless the trip is geared toward young children. You might want to test the waters with a half- or full-day excursions. Several outfitters run short trips out of Moab, Utah. For families with younger children, trips aboard larger, motorized rafts are probably safest.

If you are renting a car, don't forget to **arrange for a car seat** when you reserve. For general advice about traveling with children, consult Fodor's FYI: Travel with Your Baby (available in bookstores everywhere).

FLYING

If your children are two or older, **ask about children's airfares.** As a general rule, infants under two not occupying a seat fly at greatly reduced fares or even for free. Experts agree that it's a good idea to use safety seats aloft for children weighing less than 40 pounds. Airlines set their own policies: U.S. carriers usually require that the child be ticketed, even if he or she is young enough to ride free, since the seats must be strapped into regular seats. Do **check your airline's policy about using safety seats during takeoff and landing.** And since safety seats are not allowed everywhere in the plane, get your seat assignments early.

When reserving, **request children's meals or a freestanding bassinet** if you need them. But note that bulkhead seats, where you must sit to use the bassinet, may lack an overhead bin or storage space on the floor.

LODGING

Many hotels and most motels in Utah allow children under a certain age to stay in their parents' room at no extra charge, but others charge for them as extra adults; be sure to **find out the cutoff age for children's discounts.**

SIGHTS & ATTRACTIONS

Places that are especially appealing to children are indicated by a rubber-duckie icon (🦆) in the margin.

Consumer Protection

Whenever shopping or buying travel services in the Rockies, **pay with a major credit card,** if possible, so you can cancel payment or get reimbursed if there's a problem. If you're doing business with a particular company for the first time, **contact your local Better Business Bureau and the attorney general's offices** in your state and (for U.S. businesses) the company's home state as well. Have any complaints been filed? Finally, if you're buying a package or tour, always consider travel insurance that includes default coverage (*see* Insurance, *below*).

▶ **BBBS: Council of Better Business Bureaus** (4200 Wilson Blvd., Suite 800, Arlington, VA 22203, tel. 703/276–0100, fax 703/525–8277, www.bbb.org).

Customs & Duties

IN AUSTRALIA

Australian residents who are 18 or older may bring home $A400 worth of souvenirs and gifts (including jewelry), 250 cigarettes or 250 grams of tobacco, and 1,125 ml of alcohol (including wine, beer, and spirits). Residents under 18 may bring back $A200 worth of goods. Prohibited items include meat products. Seeds, plants, and fruits need to be declared upon arrival.

▶ **INFORMATION: Australian Customs Service** (Regional Director, Box 8, Sydney, NSW 2001, Australia, tel. 02/9213–2000, fax 02/9213–4000, www.customs.gov.au).

IN CANADA

Canadian residents who have been out of Canada for at least seven days may bring home C$750 worth of goods duty-free. If you've been away fewer than seven days but more than 48 hours, the duty-free allowance drops to C$200; if your trip lasts 24–48 hours, the allowance is C$50. You may not pool allowances with family members. Goods claimed under the C$750 exemption may follow you by mail; those claimed under the lesser exemptions must accompany you. Alcohol and tobacco products may be included in the seven-day and 48-hour exemptions but not in the 24-hour exemption. If you meet the age requirements of the province or territory through which you reenter Canada, you may bring in, duty-free, 1.14 liters (40 imperial ounces) of wine or liquor or 24 12-ounce cans or bottles of beer or ale. If you are 19 or older you may bring in, duty-free, 200 cigarettes and 50 cigars. Check ahead of time with the

Canada Customs Revenue Agency or the Department of Agriculture for policies regarding meat products, seeds, plants, and fruits.

You may send an unlimited number of gifts worth up to C$60 each duty-free to Canada. Label the package UNSOLICITED GIFT—VALUE UNDER $60. Alcohol and tobacco are excluded.

➤ **INFORMATION: Canada Customs Revenue Agency** (2265 St. Laurent Blvd. S, Ottawa, Ontario K1G 4K3, Canada, tel. 204/983–3500 or 506/636–5064; 800/461–9999 in Canada, www.ccra-adrc.gc.ca).

IN NEW ZEALAND

Homeward-bound residents 17 or older may bring back $700 worth of souvenirs and gifts. Your duty-free allowance also includes 4.5 liters of wine or beer; one 1,125-ml bottle of spirits; and either 200 cigarettes, 250 grams of tobacco, 50 cigars, or a combination of the three up to 250 grams. Prohibited items include meat products, seeds, plants, and fruits.

➤ **INFORMATION: New Zealand Customs** (Custom House, 50 Anzac Ave., Box 29, Auckland, New Zealand, tel. 09/300–5399, fax 09/359–6730, www.customs.govt.nz).

IN THE U.K.

From countries outside the European Union, including the United States, you may bring home, duty-free, 200 cigarettes or 50 cigars; 1 liter of spirits or 2 liters of fortified or sparkling wine or liqueurs; 2 liters of still table wine; 60 ml of perfume; 250 ml of toilet water; plus £145 worth of other goods, including gifts and souvenirs. If returning from outside the EU, prohibited items include meat products, seeds, plants, and fruits.

➤ **INFORMATION: HM Customs and Excise** (St. Christopher House, Southwark, London, SE1 0TE, U.K., tel. 020/7928–3344, www.hmce.gov.uk).

Dining

The restaurants we list are the cream of the crop in each price category, which is assigned based on the following chart:

CATEGORY	COST*
$$$$	over $30
$$$	$20–$30
$$	$15–$20
$	under $15

*per person for a main course at dinner, excluding drinks, service, and approximately 6½% sales tax (rates vary depending on location)

RESERVATIONS & DRESS

Reservations are always a good idea, especially when dining with a large group: we mention them only when they're essential or aren't accepted. Book as far ahead as you can, and reconfirm as soon as you arrive. We mention dress only when men are required to wear a jacket or a jacket and tie—which is rare outside of the major cities or resort areas.

Disabilities & Accessibility

Utah offers countless recreational opportunities, and travelers with disabilities should take note of them as well. Most ski areas offer adaptive ski programs—Park City Mountain Resort, for example, has excellent lesson programs—most of the U.S. Forest Service campgrounds have wheelchair-accessible sites, and many resort towns have created opportunities for all types of visitors.

➤ **LOCAL RESOURCE: Utah Travel Council** (tel. 801/538–1030).

LODGING RESERVATIONS

When discussing accessibility with an operator or reservations agent, **ask hard questions.** Are there any stairs, inside or out? Are there grab bars next to the toilet *and* in the shower/tub? How wide is the doorway to the room? To the bathroom? For the most extensive facilities meeting the latest legal specifications, **opt for newer accommodations.**

➤ **COMPLAINTS: Aviation Consumer Protection Division** (*see* Air Travel, *above*) for airline-related problems. **Civil Rights Office** (U.S. Department of Transportation, Departmental Office of Civil Rights, S-30, 400 7th St. SW, Room 10215, Washington, DC 20590, tel. 202/366–4648, fax 202/366–9371, www.dot.gov/ost/docr/index.htm) for problems with surface transportation. **Disability Rights Section** (U.S. Department of Justice, Civil Rights Division, Box 66738, Washington, DC 20035-6738, tel. 202/514–0301 or 800/514–0301; 202/514–0383 TTY; 800/514–0383 TTY, fax 202/307–1198, www.usdoj.gov/crt/ada/adahom1.htm) for general complaints.

TRAVEL AGENCIES

In the United States, the Americans with Disabilities Act requires that travel firms serve the needs of all travelers. Some agencies specialize in working with people with disabilities.

➤ **TRAVELERS WITH MOBILITY PROBLEMS: Access Adventures** (206 Chestnut Ridge Rd., Scottsville, NY 14624, tel. 716/889–9096, dltravel@prodigy.net), run by a former physical-rehabilitation counselor. **Accessible Vans of America** (9 Spielman Rd., Fairfield, NJ 07004, tel. 877/282–8267, fax 973/808–9713, www.accessiblevans.com). **CareVacations** (No. 5, 5110–50 Ave., Leduc, Alberta T9E 6V4, Canada, tel. 780/986–6404 or 877/478–7827, fax 780/986–8332, www.carevacations.com), for group tours and cruise vacations. **Flying Wheels Travel** (143 W. Bridge St., Box 382, Owatonna, MN 55060, tel. 507/451–5005 or 800/535–6790, fax 507/451–1685, www.flyingwheelstravel.com).

Discounts & Deals

Be a smart shopper and **compare all your options** before making decisions. A plane ticket bought with a promotional coupon from travel clubs, coupon books, and direct-mail offers or on the Internet may not be cheaper than the least expensive fare from a discount ticket agency. And always keep in mind that what you get is just as important as what you save.

DISCOUNT RESERVATIONS

To save money, **look into discount reservations services** with toll-free numbers, which use their buying power to get a better price on hotels, airline tickets, even car rentals. When booking a room, always **call the hotel's local toll-free number** (if one is available) rather than the central reservations number—you'll often get a better price. Always ask about special packages or corporate rates.

➤ **AIRLINE TICKETS:** tel. 800/AIR–4LESS.

➤ **HOTEL ROOMS: Accommodations Express** (tel. 800/444–7666, www.accommodationsexpress.com). **Players Express Vacations** (tel. 800/458–6161, www.playersexpress.com). **RMC Travel** (tel. 800/245–5738, www.rmcwebtravel.com). **Turbotrip.com** (tel. 800/473–7829, www.turbotrip.com).

PACKAGE DEALS

Don't confuse packages and guided tours. When you buy a package, you travel on your own, just as though you had planned the trip yourself. Fly/drive packages, which combine airfare and car rental, are often a good deal.

Emergencies

➤ **SALT LAKE CITY HOSPITALS: Columbia St. Mark's Hospital** (1200 E. 3900 South St., tel. 801/268–7111). **Salt Lake Regional Medical Center** (1050 E. South Temple St., tel. 801/350–4111). **LDS Hospital** (8th Ave. and C St., tel. 801/408–1100). **Primary Children's Medical Center** (100 N. Medical Dr., tel. 801/588–2000). **University Hospital and Clinics** (50 N. Medical Dr., tel. 801/581–2121).

➤ **SALT LAKE CITY PHARMACIES: Broadway Pharmacy** (242 E. 300 South St., tel. 801/363–3939). **Harmon's Supermarket** (3270 S. 1300 East St., tel. 801/487–5461).

➤ **WASATCH FRONT HOSPITALS: Logan Regional Hospital** (1400 N. 500 East St., Logan, tel. 435/752–2050). **Columbia-Ogden Regional Medical Center** (5475 S. 500 East St., Ogden, tel. 801/479–2111). **Family Health and Emergency Center** (1665 Bonanza Dr., Park City, tel. 435/649–7640). **Utah Valley Regional Medical Center** (1034 N. 500 West St., Provo, tel. 801/373–7850).

Gay & Lesbian Travel

Most resort towns are progressive and gay-friendly. For details about the gay and lesbian scene, consult *Fodor's Gay Guide to the USA* (available in bookstores everywhere).

➤ **GAY- & LESBIAN-FRIENDLY TRAVEL AGENCIES: Different Roads Travel** (8383 Wilshire Blvd., Suite 902, Beverly Hills, CA 90211, tel. 323/651–5557 or 800/429–8747, fax 323/651–3678, lgernert@tzell.com). **Kennedy Travel** (314 Jericho Turnpike, Floral Park, NY 11001, tel. 516/352–4888 or 800/237–7433, fax 516/354–8849, www.kennedytravel.com). **Now Voyager** (4406 18th St., San Francisco, CA 94114, tel. 415/626–1169 or 800/255–6951, fax 415/626–8626, www.nowvoyager.com). **Skylink Travel and Tour** (1006 Mendocino Ave., Santa Rosa, CA 95401, tel. 707/546–9888 or 800/225–5759, fax 707/546–9891, www.skylinktravel.com), serving lesbian travelers.

Guidebooks

Plan well and you won't be sorry. Guidebooks are excellent tools—and you can take them with you. You may want to check out the *Compass American Guide* to Utah, which is thorough on culture and history and includes color photographs.

Holidays

Major national holidays include New Year's Day (Jan. 1); Martin Luther King, Jr., Day (3rd Mon. in Jan.); Presidents Day (3rd Mon. in Feb.); Memorial Day (last Mon. in May); Independence Day (July 4); Labor Day (1st Mon. in Sept.); Thanksgiving Day (4th

Thurs. in Nov.); Christmas Eve and Christmas Day (Dec. 24 and 25); and New Year's Eve (Dec. 31). July 24 is Pioneer Day, with celebrations throughout Utah. Businesses in cities respect these, while resort town retailers often extend their hours.

Insurance

The most useful travel-insurance plan is a comprehensive policy that includes coverage for trip cancellation and interruption, default, trip delay, and medical expenses (with a waiver for pre-existing conditions).

Without insurance you will lose all or most of your money if you cancel your trip, regardless of the reason. Default insurance covers you if your tour operator, airline, or cruise line goes out of business. Trip-delay covers expenses that arise because of bad weather or mechanical delays. Study the fine print when comparing policies.

Always **buy travel policies directly from the insurance company**; if you buy them from a cruise line, airline, or tour operator that goes out of business you probably will not be covered for the agency or operator's default, a major risk. Before making any purchase, **review your existing health and home-owner's policies** to find what they cover away from home.

➤ **TRAVEL INSURERS:** In the U.S.: **Access America** (6600 W. Broad St., Richmond, VA 23230, tel. 800/284–8300, fax 804/673–1491, www.etravelprotection.com), **Travel Guard International** (1145 Clark St., Stevens Point, WI 54481, tel. 715/345–0505 or 800/826–1300, fax 800/955–8785, www.travelguard.com).

For International Travelers

For information on customs restrictions, *see* Customs & Duties, *above.*

CURRENCY

The dollar is the basic unit of U.S. currency. It has 100 cents. Coins include the copper penny (1¢); the silvery nickel (5¢), dime (10¢), quarter (25¢), and half-dollar (50¢); and the golden $1 coin, replacing a now-rare silver dollar. Bills are denominated $1, $5, $10, $20, $50, and $100, all green and identical in size; designs vary.

ELECTRICITY

The U.S. standard is AC, 110 volts/60 cycles. Plugs have two flat pins set parallel to each other.

EMERGENCIES

For police, fire, or ambulance, **dial 911** (0 in rural areas).

INSURANCE

Britons and Australians need extra medical coverage when traveling overseas.

➤ **INSURANCE INFORMATION:** In the U.K.: **Association of British Insurers** (51–55 Gresham St., London EC2V 7HQ, U.K., tel. 020/7600–3333, fax 020/7696–8999, www.abi.org.uk). In Australia: **Insurance Council of Australia** (Level 3, 56 Pitt St., Sydney NSW 2000, tel. 02/9253–5100, fax 02/9253–5111, www.ica.com.au). In Canada: **RBC Insurance** (6880 Financial Dr., Mississauga, Ontario L5N 7Y5, Canada, tel. 905/816–2400 or 800/668–4342 in Canada, fax 905/816–2498, www.royalbank.com). In New Zealand: **Insurance Council of New Zealand** (Level 7, 111–115 Customhouse Quay, Box 474, Wellington, New Zealand, tel. 04/472–5230, fax 04/473–3011, www.icnz.org.nz).

MAIL & SHIPPING

You can buy stamps and aerograms and send letters and parcels in post offices. Stamp-dispensing machines can occasionally be found in airports, bus and train stations, office buildings, drugstores, and the like. You can also deposit mail in the stout, dark blue, steel bins at strategic locations everywhere and in the mail chutes of large buildings; pickup schedules are posted.

For mail sent within the United States, you need a 34¢ stamp for first-class letters weighing up to 1 ounce (23¢ for each additional ounce) and 21¢ for domestic postcards. For overseas mail, you pay 80¢ for 1-ounce airmail letters, 70¢ for airmail postcards, and 35¢ for surface-rate postcards. For Canada and Mexico you need a 60¢ stamp for a 1-ounce letter and 50¢ for a postcard. For 70¢ you can buy an aerogram—a single sheet of lightweight blue paper that folds into its own envelope, stamped for overseas airmail.

To receive mail on the road, have it sent c/o General Delivery at your destination's main post office (use the correct five-digit zip code). You must pick up mail in person within 30 days and show a driver's license or passport.

PASSPORTS & VISAS

When traveling internationally, **carry your passport** even if you don't need one (it's always the best form of I.D.) and **make two photocopies of the data page** (one for someone at home and another for you, carried separately from your passport). If you lose your passport, promptly call the nearest embassy or consulate and the local police.

Visitor visas are not necessary for Canadian citizens, or for citizens of Australia and the United Kingdom who are staying less than 90 days.

➤ **AUSTRALIAN CITIZENS: Australian Passport Office** (tel. 131–232). **U.S. Office of Australia Affairs** (MLC Centre, 19–29 Martin Pl., 59th floor, Sydney NSW 2000, Australia).

➤ **CANADIAN CITIZENS: Passport Office** (tel. 819/994–3500; 800/567–6868 in Canada).

➤ **NEW ZEALAND CITIZENS: New Zealand Passport Office** (tel. 04/494–0700 for application procedures; 0800/225–050 in New Zealand for application-status updates). **U.S. Office of New Zealand Affairs** (29 Fitzherbert Terr., Thorndon, Wellington, New Zealand).

➤ **U.K. CITIZENS: London Passport Office** (tel. 0870/521–0410) for application procedures and emergency passports. **U.S. Embassy Visa Information Line** (tel. 01891/200–290). **U.S. Embassy Visa Branch** (5 Upper Grosvenor Sq., London W1A 1AE, U.K.); send a self-addressed, stamped envelope. **U.S. Consulate General** (Queen's House, Queen St., Belfast BTI 6EO, Northern Ireland).

TELEPHONES

All U.S. telephone numbers consist of a three-digit area code and a seven-digit local number. Within most local calling areas, dial only the seven-digit number. To call between area-code regions, dial "1" then all 10 digits; the same goes for calls to numbers prefixed by "800," "888," and "877"—all toll-free. For calls to numbers preceded by "900" you must pay—usually dearly.

For international calls, dial "011" followed by the country code and the local number. For help, dial "0" and ask for an overseas operator. The country code is 61 for Australia, 64 for New Zealand, 44 for the United Kingdom. Calling Canada is the same as calling within the United States. Most local phone books list country codes and U.S. area codes. The country code for the United States is 1.

For operator assistance, dial "0." To obtain someone's phone number, call directory assistance, 555–1212 or occasionally 411 (free at public phones). To have the person you're calling foot the bill, phone collect; dial "0" instead of "1" before the 10-digit number.

At pay phones, instructions are usually posted. Usually you insert coins in a slot (10¢–35¢ for local calls) and wait for a steady tone before dialing. When you call long-distance, the operator will tell you how much to insert; prepaid phone cards, widely available in various denominations, are easier. Call the number on the back, punch in the card's personal identification number when prompted, then dial your number.

Lodging

Assume that hotels operate on the **European Plan** (EP, with no meals) unless we specify that they use the **Breakfast Plan** (BP, with a full breakfast), **Continental Plan** (CP, with a Continental breakfast), **Modified American Plan** (MAP, with breakfast and dinner), or the **Full American Plan** (FAP, with all meals).

The lodgings we list are the cream of the crop in each price category. We always list the facilities that are available—but we don't specify whether they cost extra: When pricing accommodations, always ask what's included and what costs extra. All hotels listed have private bath unless otherwise noted. Price categories are based on the following chart:

CATEGORY	COST*
$$$$	over $225
$$$	$150–$225
$$	$75–$150
$	under $75

Prices are for a standard double room in high season, not including the 4% tax and service.

➤ **GENERAL INFORMATION: Utah Hotel and Lodging Association** (9 Exchange Pl., Suite 115, Salt Lake City, UT 84114, tel. 801/359-0104).

APARTMENT & VILLA RENTALS

If you want a home base that's roomy enough for a family and comes with cooking facilities, **consider a furnished rental.** These can save you money, especially if you're traveling with a group. Home-exchange directories sometimes list rentals as well as exchanges. Also see the A to Z sections in the state chapters for local businesses that arrange cabin, house, and condo rentals.

➤ **INTERNATIONAL AGENTS: Hideaways International** (767 Islington St., Portsmouth, NH 03801, tel. 603/430-4433 or 800/

843–4433, fax 603/430–4444, www.hideaways.com; membership $129).

B&BS AND INNS

Charm is the long suit of these establishments, which generally occupy a restored older building with some historical or architectural significance. They're generally small, with fewer than 20 rooms, and located outside cities. Breakfast is usually included in the rates.

➤ **INFORMATION: Bed & Breakfast Inns of Utah** (Box 2639, Park City, UT 84060, fax 801/595–0332, www.bbin.com).

CAMPING

Across the Wasatch–Cache and Uinta national forests are a number of wonderful campgrounds. Between Big and Little Cottonwood canyons there are four higher-elevation sites. Of the nine facilities in Logan Canyon, Guinavah-Malibu and Tony Grove campgrounds are the nicest. Near Nephi a pair of campgrounds are found along the Nebo Loop Scenic Byway. All 11 campgrounds in the Huntsville area up Ogden Canyon offer swimming and fishing.

In the vicinity of Provo, American Fork, Provo Canyon, and the Hobble Creek drainage there are dozens of possibilities. In Sanpete County, most campground facilities are found to the east in the Manti–La Sal National Forest. Additional campgrounds are at the region's state parks and national monuments and at the Little Sahara Recreation Area.

Sites range from rustic (pit toilets and cold running water) to posh, with hot showers, swimming pools, paved trailer pads that can accommodate even jumbo RVs, and full hookups. Fees vary, from $6 to $10 a night for tents and up to $21 for RVs, but are usually waived once the water is turned off for the winter.

Sometimes site reservations are accepted, and then only for up to seven days (early birds reserve up to a year in advance); more often, they're not. Campers who prefer a more remote setting may camp in the backcountry; it's free but you might need a permit, available from park visitor centers and ranger stations.

➤ **INFORMATION: U.S. Forest Service** (tel. 800/280–2267 for reservations).

HOME EXCHANGES

If you would like to exchange your home for someone else's, **join a home-exchange organization,** which will send you its updated listings of available exchanges for a year and will include your own listing in at least one of them. It's up to you to make specific arrangements.

➤ **EXCHANGE CLUBS: HomeLink International** (Box 47747, Tampa, FL 33647, tel. 813/975–9825 or 800/638–3841, fax 813/910–8144, www.homelink.org; $106 per year). **Intervac U.S.** (Box 590504, San Francisco, CA 94159, tel. 800/756–4663, fax 415/435–7440, www.intervacus.com; $93 yearly fee includes one catalogue and on-line access).

HOSTELS

No matter what your age, you can **save on lodging costs by staying at hostels.** In some 4,500 locations in more than 70 countries around the world, Hostelling International (HI), the umbrella group for a number of national youth-hostel associations, offers single-sex, dorm-style beds and, at many hostels, rooms for couples and family accommodations. Membership in any HI national hostel association, open to travelers of all ages, allows you to stay in HI-affiliated hostels at member rates; one-year membership is about $25 for adults (C$26.75 in Canada, £9.30 in the U.K., $30 in Australia, and $30 in New Zealand); hostels run about $10–$25 per night. Members have priority if the hostel is full; they're also eligible for discounts around the world, even on rail and bus travel in some countries.

➤ **ORGANIZATIONS: Hostelling International—American Youth Hostels** (733 15th St. NW, Suite 840, Washington, DC 20005, tel. 202/783–6161, fax 202/783–6171, www.hiayh.org). **Hostelling International—Canada** (400–205 Catherine St., Ottawa, Ontario K2P 1C3, Canada, tel. 613/237–7884; 800/663–5777 in Canada, fax 613/237–7868, www.hostellingintl.ca). **Youth Hostel Association of England and Wales** (Trevelyan House, 8 St. Stephen's Hill, St. Albans, Hertfordshire AL1 2DY, U.K., tel. 0870/8708808, fax 01727/844126, www.yha.org.uk). **Youth Hostel Association Australia** (10 Mallett St., Camperdown, NSW 2050, Australia, tel. 02/9565–1699, fax 02/9565–1325, www.yha.com.au). **Youth Hostels Association of New Zealand** (Level 3, 193 Cashel St., Box 436, Christchurch, New Zealand, tel. 03/379–9970, fax 03/365–4476, www.yha.org.nz).

HOTELS

Most urban hotels cater to business travelers, with restaurants, cocktail lounges, pools, exercise equipment, meeting rooms— and rates that reflect the range of amenities. Less expensive hotels are clean and comfortable but have fewer facilities. All-suites hotels give you more room for the money; examples include Courtyard by Marriott and Embassy Suites. Resorts can be more deluxe, with every imaginable amenity. Rural lodgings are generally simple (sometimes rustic).

Many properties offer special weekend rates, sometimes up to 50% off regular prices. These deals are usually not available in peak season, however, when hotels are normally full. The same discounts generally hold true for resorts in the off-seasons.

➤ **TOLL-FREE NUMBERS: Best Western** (tel. 800/528–1234, www.bestwestern.com). **Choice** (tel. 800/221–2222, www.choicehotels.com). **Colony** (tel. 800/777–1700, www.colony.com). **Comfort** (tel. 800/228–5150, www.comfortinn.com). **Days Inn** (tel. 800/325–2525, www.daysinn.com). **Doubletree and Red Lion Hotels** (tel. 800/222–8733, www.doubletree.com). **Embassy Suites** (tel. 800/

362–2779, www.embassysuites.com). **Fairfield Inn** (tel. 800/228–2800, www.marriott.com). **Hilton** (tel. 800/445–8667, www.hilton.com). **Holiday Inn** (tel. 800/465–4329, www.basshotels.com). **Howard Johnson** (tel. 800/654–4656, www.hojo.com). **Hyatt Hotels & Resorts** (tel. 800/233–1234, www.hyatt.com). **La Quinta** (tel. 800/531–5900, www.laquinta.com). **Marriott** (tel. 800/228–9290, www.marriott.com). **Radisson** (tel. 800/333–3333, www.radisson.com). **Ramada** (tel. 800/228–2828, www.ramada.com). **Sheraton** (tel. 800/325–3535, www.starwoodhotels.com). **Westin Hotels & Resorts** (tel. 800/228–3000, www.westin.com).

Money Matters

First-class hotel rooms in Salt Lake City cost from $75 to $175 a night, although some "value" hotel rooms go for $40–$60, and, as elsewhere in the United States, rooms in national budget chain motels go for around $40 nightly. As a rule, costs outside the major cities are lower, except in the deluxe resorts. A cup of coffee costs between 50¢ and $1, the price for a hamburger runs between $3 and $5, and a beer at a bar is between $1.50 and $3; expect to pay double in resort towns.

Prices throughout this guide are given for adults. Substantially reduced fees are almost always available for children, students, and senior citizens. The sales taxes in Utah is 4.75%.

CREDIT CARDS
Throughout this guide, the following abbreviations are used: **AE,** American Express; **D,** Discover; **DC,** Diners Club; **MC,** MasterCard; and **V,** Visa.

Outdoors & Sports

Utah is one of America's greatest playgrounds, and many residents make exercise a high priority. Regardless of the outdoor activity or your level of skill, safety must come first. Remember: **know your limits!**

Respect area rules and closures, as well as the admonition **leave only footprints, take only pictures.** Many areas are open only to hikers, with vehicles, mountain bikes, and horses banned. All archaeological artifacts, including rock etchings and paintings, are protected by federal law and must be left untouched and undisturbed. Locals can be strident about protecting their wilderness, and they take recycling seriously; you'll be unpopular if you litter or fail to recycle your cans and bottles.

BACKCOUNTRY SKIING

Avalanche risks make backcountry skiing ill-advised for all but those with the proper safety equipment and considerable experience. The guided Ski Utah Interconnect Adventure Tour is a combination of lift-service and backcountry skiing in Utah's three major skiing regions: Big Cottonwood, Little Cottonwood, and Park City. Much of the trip is within resort boundaries, and it can be negotiated either on telemark skis or with regular alpine gear. The fee is $150, including lunch and transportation.

Strong intermediate and advanced skiers can also enjoy heliskiing, whether in search of powder or the solitude of the backcountry. Wasatch Powderbird Guides has permits for several thousand acres of skiable terrain, mostly in the basins and drainages on the periphery of Alta and Snowbird. Tours cost $500–$600 per person per day, and reservations are required.

➤ **CONTACTS: Ski Utah Interconnect Adventure Tour** (c/o Ski Utah, 150 W. 500 South St., Salt Lake City 84101, tel. 801/534–1907). **Wasatch Powderbird Guides** (Box 920057, Snowbird 84092, tel. 801/742–2800.)

CYCLING

High, rugged country puts a premium on fitness. Even if you can ride 40 mi at home without breaking a sweat, you might find yourself struggling terribly on steep climbs and in elevations often exceeding 10,000 ft. If you have an extended tour in mind, arrive a couple of days early and try some shorter rides just to **acclimatize yourself to the altitude and terrain.**

Although the valleys may be scorching, high-mountain passes may still be lined with snow in summer. Pack accordingly. (Bicycle racers often stuff newspaper inside their jerseys when descending from high passes to shield themselves from the chill.) Although you shouldn't have much problem renting a bike, bring your own helmut and sturdy cycling shoes (or interlocking shoe-and-pedal system). If bring your own bike, be prepared to spend as much as $150 in special luggage handling.

Guided trips cost between $80 and $150 a day, depending on lodging and meals. The Adventure Cycling Association is perhaps the best general source of information on biking in the Rockies—with detailed maps and information on trip organizers. When you're in a resort town, check with the mountain to see if they offer lift-serviced mountain biking.

➤ **CONTACTS: Adventure Cycling Association** (Box 8308, Missoula, MT 59807, tel. 406/721–1776 or 800/755–2453, www.adventurecycling.org).

KAYAKING

Steep mountains and narrow canyons usually mean fast-flowing water in which the maneuverability of kayaks is a great asset. A means of transport for less experienced paddlers is the inflatable kayak.

To minimize environmental impact, a reservation policy is used for many rivers of the West. Often, the reserved times—many of the *prime* times—are prebooked by licensed outfitters, limiting your possibilities if you're planning a self-guided trip. Unless you can be flexible about when and where to go, it's best to **sign on with a guided trip.** Dvorak Expeditions leads trips on the rivers of eastern Utah and conducts clinics, including certification courses, for kayakers of all abilities. River Travel

Center arranges trips in Utah, among other destinations. Costs start at $100 a day.

Outfitters provide life jackets, paddles, and helmets; they often throw in waterproof containers for cameras, clothing, and sleeping bags. Bring bug repellent, a good hat, water-resistant sandals or old sneakers, and sunblock. The sun on the river can be intense, but once it disappears behind canyon walls, the temperature can drop 30° or more, so packing warm clothing is a good idea.

➤ **INSTRUCTION AND TRIPS: Dvorak Expeditions** (17921 U.S. 285, Nathrop, CO 81236, tel. 800/824–3795). **River Travel Center** (Box 6, Point Arena, CA 95468, tel. 800/882–7238).

FISHING

Field and Stream magazine is a leading source of information on fishing travel, technique, and equipment. Fishing licenses are required; they're available at tackle shops and a variety of local stores. Tribal fishing licenses are necessary on reservation land.

The seasons may vary from region to region, and from species to species. A few streams are considered "private" in that they are stocked by a local club; other rivers are fly-fishing or catch-and-release only, so be sure you know the rules. Water can be cold, especially at higher elevations, so **wear waterproof waders.** Outfitters and some tackle shops rent equipment, but you're best off bringing your own gear. Lures are another story, though: whether you plan to fish with flies or other lures, the staff at local tackle shops knows what works best.

For lists of guides, contact the state tourism department. A guide will cost about $250 per day and can be shared by two anglers if they're fishing from a boat and possibly by three if they're wading. Lunch will probably be included, and flies might be, although there may be an extra $15–$20 charge for these.

➤ **INFORMATION AND LICENSES: Utah Division of Wildlife Resources** (1596 W. North Temple St., Salt Lake City, UT 84116, tel. 801/538–4700).

➤ **INSTRUCTION: Jan's Mountain Outfitters** (1600 Park Ave., Box 280, Park City, UT 84060, tel. 801/649–4949 or 800/745–1020).

HIKING

Although guided-trip costs can be as little as $30 a day, many people organize their own treks. *Backpacker* magazine is the leading national hiking publication, and there are also many regional publications. **Get a hiking guidebook.** Most such books provide fairly detailed trail descriptions, including distances and elevation gains involved and recommended side trips. Falcon Books publishes hiking guides to areas throughout the Rockies.

If you plan to hike where trails might not be well marked or maintained, you'll need not only a hiking guidebook, but also maps and a compass. Maps in several scales are available from the U.S. Geological Survey; request the survey's free index and catalog so you can choose what you need. Topographical maps are also available through the U.S. Forest Service, the U.S. Bureau of Land Management, and many well-equipped outdoors stores.

To take you into the wilds, boots should have thick soles and plenty of ankle support; if your shoes are new and you plan to spend much time on the trail, break them in at home. Bring a day pack for short hikes, along with a canteen or water bottle, and don't forget rain gear, a hat, sunscreen, and insect repellent.

➤ **CONTACTS: American Hiking Society** (Box 20160, Washington, DC 20041, tel. 301/565–6704). **U.S. Geological Survey** (Distribution Section, Box 25286, Federal Center, Denver, CO 80225, tel. 303/202–4700 or 888/275–8747).

▶ **HIKING MAPS AND GUIDES:** Adventurous Traveler Bookstore (tel. 802/860–6667 or 800/282–3963). **Falcon Books** (tel. 800/725–8303). **The Mountaineers** (300 3rd Ave. W, Seattle, WA 98119, tel. 206/284–6310). **Sierra Club Books** (85 2nd St., 4th floor, San Francisco, CA 94105, tel. 415/977–5500). **U.S. Bureau of Land Management** (tel. 303/239–3600).

NATIONAL PARKS

Look into discount passes to save money on park entrance fees. The National Parks Pass ($50) gets you and your companions free admission to all parks for one year. (Camping and parking are extra.) A percentage of the proceeds from sales of the pass will fund National Parks projects. Both the Golden Age Passport ($10), for those 62 and older, and the Golden Access Passport (free), for travelers with disabilities, entitle holders to free entry to all national parks, plus 50% off fees for the use of many park facilities and services. You must show proof of age and of U.S. citizenship or permanent residency (such as a U.S. passport, driver's license, or birth certificate) and, if requesting Golden Access, proof of disability. The Golden Age and Golden Access passes are available at all national parks wherever entrance fees are charged. The National Parks Pass is available by mail or through the Internet.

▶ **PASSES BY MAIL: National Park Service** (National Park Service/Department of Interior, 1849 C St. NW, Washington, DC 20240, tel. 202/208–4747, www.nps.gov). **National Parks Pass** (27540 Ave. Mentry, Valencia, CA 91355, tel. 888/GO–PARKS, www.nationalparks.org).

RAFTING

Unless you are a white-water expert, it's best to organize a trip through a recognized outfitter. Even then, you should be a good swimmer and in solid general health. Different companies are licensed to run different rivers, although there may be several companies working the same river. Some organizers combine river rafting with other activities: pack trips, mountain-biking, hiking, or fishing.

"Raft" can mean any many things: an inflated raft in which passengers do the paddling; an inflated raft or wooden dory in which a licensed professional does the work; a motorized raft on which some oar work might be required. Be sure you **know what kind of raft you'll be riding**—or paddling—before booking a trip.

Day trips typically run between $30 and $60 per person. Expect to pay between $80 and $120 per day for multiday trips. Raft Utah publishes a comprehensive directory with full descriptions of all of Utah's rivers and the outfitters who run them.

➤ **OUTFITTER LISTINGS: Raft Utah** (tel. 800/200–1160).

➤ **OUTFITTERS: Adrift Adventures** (Box 192, Jensen, UT 84035, tel. 800/824–0150). **Mountain Travel/Sobek** (6420 Fairmount Ave., El Cerrito, CA 94530, tel. 888/687–6235). **OARS** (Box 67, Angels Camp, CA 95222, tel. 800/346–6277).

ROCK CLIMBING

Climbing is a team sport, so **don't overestimate your capabilities** or you'll endanger not only yourself but other team members. Before you sign on with a trip, discuss your climbing skills, experience, and physical condition with the outfitter. A fair self-assessment of your abilities also helps a guide choose appropriate climbing routes, which are rated according to their difficulty. You may want to get in some instruction and training time at a climbing wall before your trip.

Guide services, outfitters, and some outdoors stores rent helmets, pitons, ropes, and axes—usually on a per-item, per-day basis. Be sure to ask your guide what other equipment and supplies you'll need to bring. Temperatures can fluctuate dramatically at higher elevations. Bringing several thin layers of clothing, including a sturdy, waterproof/breathable outer shell.

Organized trip costs depend on group size, length of climb, instruction rendered, and equipment supplied. Count on spending at least $80 a day, though a small-group multiday instructional climb can push $200 a day. The American Alpine Institute leads trips around the world, ranging from training climbs to expeditionary first ascents. It's one of the nation's most respected climbing organizations.

➤ **INSTRUCTIONAL PROGRAMS AND OUTFITTERS: American Alpine Institute** (1515 12th St., N-4, Bellingham, WA 98225, tel. 360/671–1505). **The Wilderness School** (72 W. 500 North St., Orem, UT 84057, tel. 801/221–0398, www.highangletechnologies. com).

Packing

Informality reigns here; jeans, sport shirts, and T-shirts fit in almost everywhere, for both men and women. The few restaurants and performing-arts events where dressier outfits are required, usually in resorts and larger cities, are the exception. You'll also want to dress conservatively if you attend events at Native American reservations—skirts or long pants for women, long pants for men.

Wear sunglasses and a sun hat at high altitudes; the thinner atmosphere requires sunscreen with a greater SPF than you might need at lower elevations. For walks and hikes, you'll need sturdy footwear.

In summer you'll want shorts during the day. But because early mornings and nights can be cold, and high passes windy, **choose clothing appropriate for chilly and wet weather.** Cotton clothing, including denim—although fine on warm, dry days—can be uncomfortable when it gets cold or rains. Try layering—a T-shirt under another shirt under a waterproof jacket—and peel off layers as you go. **In winter prepare for subzero temperatures** with good boots, warm socks and liners, long johns, a well-insulated jacket, and a warm hat and mittens. Clothing made of wool is ideal, though bulky. There are now a number of new synthetics that provide warmth without bulk and maintain their insulating properties even when wet.

In your carry-on luggage **pack an extra pair of eyeglasses or contact lenses and enough of any medication** you take to last the entire trip. You may also ask your doctor to write a spare prescription using the drug's generic name, since brand names may vary from country to country. In luggage to be checked, **never pack prescription drugs or valuables.** To avoid customs delays, carry medications in their original packaging. And don't forget to carry with you the addresses of offices that handle refunds of lost traveler's checks. Check *Fodor's How to Pack* (available in bookstores everywhere) for more tips.

CHECKING LUGGAGE

How many carry-on bags you can bring with you is up to the airline. Most allow two, but not always, so make sure that everything you carry aboard will fit under your seat or in the overhead bin, and get to the gate early. Note that if you have a seat at the back of the plane, you'll probably board first, while the overhead bins are still empty.

If you are flying internationally, note that baggage allowances may be determined not by piece but by weight—generally 88 pounds (40 kilograms) in first class, 66 pounds (30 kilograms) in business class, and 44 pounds (20 kilograms) in economy.

Airline liability for baggage is limited to $1,250 per person on flights within the United States. On international flights it amounts to $9.07 per pound or $20 per kilogram for checked baggage (roughly $640 per 70-pound bag) and $400 per passenger for unchecked baggage. You can buy additional coverage at check-in for about $10 per $1,000 of coverage, but it excludes a rather extensive list of items, shown on your airline ticket.

Before departure, **itemize your bags' contents** and their worth, and label the bags with your name, address, and phone number. (If you use your home address, cover it so potential thieves can't see it readily.) Inside each bag, **pack a copy of your itinerary.** At check-in, **make sure that each bag is correctly tagged with the** destination airport's three-letter code. If your bags arrive damaged or fail to arrive at all, file a written report with the airline before leaving the airport.

Safety

Many trails are at high altitudes, where oxygen is scarce. They're also frequently desolate. **Carry emergency supplies.** Proper equipment includes a flashlight, a compass, waterproof matches, a first-aid kit, a knife, and a light plastic tarp. Backcountry skiers should add a repair kit, a blanket, an avalanche beacon, and a lightweight shovel to their lists. Always **bring extra food and a canteen of water,** as dehydration is a common occurrence at high altitudes. **Never drink from streams or lakes** unless you boil the water first or purify it with tablets. Giardia, an intestinal parasite, may be present. Although Lyme disease isn't a problem in Utah, some ticks carry Rocky Mountain spotted fever. **Use a good insect repellent.**

Always **check the condition of roads and trails, and get the latest weather reports** before setting out. In summer **take precautions against heat stroke or exhaustion** by resting frequently in shaded areas; in winter **take precautions against hypothermia** by layering clothing. Ultimately, proper planning, common sense, and good physical conditioning are the strongest guards against the elements.

ALTITUDE

You may feel dizzy and weak and find yourself breathing heavily—signs that the thin mountain air isn't giving you your accustomed dose of oxygen. Take it easy and **rest often for a few days until you're acclimatized.** Throughout your stay drink plenty of water and watch your alcohol consumption. If you experience severe headaches and nausea, see a doctor. The remedy for altitude-related discomfort is to go down quickly into heavier air. Other altitude-related problems include dehydration and overexposure to the sun due to the thin air.

WILD ANIMALS

Although a herd of grazing elk or a bighorn sheep high on a hillside is most certainly a Kodak moment, an encounter with a bear or mountain lion is not. Always hike in groups, make plenty of noise, and keep dogs on a leash and small children between adults. While camping, store all food, utensils, and clothing with food odors far away from your tent, preferably high in a tree. If you encounter a bear or big cat, do not run. For bears, back away quietly; for lions, make yourself look as big as possible. In either case be prepared to fend off the animal with loud noises, rocks, sticks, etc. And, as the saying goes, **do not feed the bears**—or any wild animals, dangerous or not.

Keep a lookout for rattlesnakes. You're likely not to have any problems if you maintain distance from snakes that you see— they can strike only half of their length, so a 6-ft clearance should allow you to stay unharmed, especially if you don't provoke them. If you're bitten, don't panic. Just get to a hospital within two to three hours. Roughly 30% to 40% of bites are dry bites, where the snake uses no venom (still, get thee to a hospital). Avoid hiking at night when snakes are on the prowl and less visible. You may want to **pick up a kit called the Extractor for use if bitten;** the kits are sold in major sporting-goods stores.

Senior-Citizen Travel

To qualify for age-related discounts, **mention your senior-citizen status up front** when booking hotel reservations (not when checking out) and before you're seated in restaurants (not when paying the bill). When renting a car, ask about promotional car-rental discounts, which can be cheaper than senior-citizen rates.

➤ **EDUCATIONAL PROGRAMS: Elderhostel** (11 Ave. de Lafayette, Boston, MA 02111-1746, tel. 877/426–8056, fax 877/426–2166, www.elderhostel.org).

Sightseeing Guides

Innsbrook Tours provides tours of Salt Lake City, Great Salt Lake, and the Bingham Canyon Copper Mine; most trips include lunch at Brigham Young's historic living quarters. Lewis Brothers Stages conducts tours of city sights in *Old Salty*, an open-air, rubber-tire train. Tours depart from Temple and Trolley squares. Utah Heritage Foundation offers the most authoritative tours of Salt Lake's historic sights.

► **CONTACTS: Innsbrook Tours** (3353 S. Main St., Salt Lake City, tel. 801/534–1001). **Lewis Brothers Stages** (549 W. 500 South St., Salt Lake City, tel. 801/359–8677 or 800/826–5844). **Utah Heritage Foundation** (485 Canyon Rd., Salt Lake City, tel. 801/533–0858).

Telephones

AREA & COUNTRY CODES

The area codes for Utah are 801 and 435.

LOCAL CALLS

Pay telephones cost 35¢ for local calls. Charge phones, also common, may be used to charge a call to a telephone-company calling card or a credit card, or for collect calls.

Many hotels place a surcharge on local calls made from your room and include a service charge on long-distance calls. It may be cheaper for you to make your calls from a pay phone in the hotel lobby rather than from your room.

Time

Utah is in the Mountain Time Zone, which is two hours earlier than Eastern time and one hour later than Pacific time. It is one hour earlier than Chicago, seven hours earlier than London, and 17 hours earlier than Sydney.

Tipping

It's customary to tip 15% at restaurants; 20% in resort towns is not only appreciated, but expected. For coat checks and bellman, $1 per coat or bag is the minimum. Taxi drivers expect 10% to 15% percent, depending on where you are. In resort towns, remember to tip other service workers such as ski technicians, sandwich makers, coffee baristas, and the like—a few dollars here go a long way toward improved service.

Tours & Packages

Because everything is prearranged on a prepackaged tour or independent vacation, you spend less time planning—and often get it all at a good price.

BOOKING WITH AN AGENT

Travel agents are excellent resources. But it's a good idea to collect brochures from several agencies as some agents' suggestions may be influenced by relationships with tour and package firms that reward them for volume sales. If you have a special interest, **find an agent with expertise in that area**; the American Society of Travel Agents (ASTA; *see* Travel Agencies, *below*) has a database of specialists worldwide.

Make sure your travel agent knows the accommodations and other services of the place being recommended. Ask about the hotel's location, room size, beds, and whether it has a pool, room service, or programs for children, if you care about these. Has your agent been there in person or sent others whom you can contact?

Do some homework on your own, too: local tourism boards can provide information about lesser-known and small-niche operators, some of which may sell only direct.

BUYER BEWARE

Each year consumers are stranded or lose their money when tour operators—even large ones with excellent reputations—go out of business. So **check out the operator.** Ask several travel agents about its reputation, and try to **book with a company that has a consumer-protection program.** (Look for information in the company's brochure.) In the United States, members of the National Tour Association and the United States Tour Operators Association are required to set aside funds to cover your payments and travel arrangements in the event that the company defaults. It's also a good idea to choose a company that participates in the American Society of Travel Agents' Tour Operator Program (TOP); ASTA will act as mediator in any disputes between you and your tour operator.

Remember that the more your package or tour includes the better you can predict the ultimate cost of your vacation. Make sure you know exactly what is covered, and **beware of hidden costs.** Are taxes, tips, and transfers included? Entertainment and excursions? These can add up.

➤ **TOUR-OPERATOR RECOMMENDATIONS: American Society of Travel Agents** (*see* Travel Agencies, *below*). **National Tour Association** (NTA; 546 E. Main St., Lexington, KY 40508, tel. 859/226–4444 or 800/682–8886, www.ntaonline.com). **United States Tour Operators Association** (USTOA; 342 Madison Ave., Suite 1522, New York, NY 10173, tel. 212/599–6599 or 800/468–7862, fax 212/599–6744, www.ustoa.com).

Train Travel

Amtrak connects the Rockies to both coasts and all major American cities with trains that run through Salt Lake City. The company also has service to Ogden and Provo.

On the Heber Valley Historic Railroad you can catch the *Heber Creeper*, a turn-of-the-20th-century steam-engine train that rides the rails from Heber City across Heber Valley, alongside Deer Creek Reservoir, down Provo Canyon to Vivian Park.

➤ **CONTACTS: Amtrak** (tel. 800/872–7245, www.amtrak.com).
Heber Valley Historic Railroad (450 S. 600 West St., Heber City
UT 84032, tel. 435/654–5601).

Transportation Around Salt Lake City and the Wasatch

Finding your way around Salt Lake City and other Wasatch Front
cities is easy, largely because early Mormon settlers laid out all
the towns in grids. In Salt Lake, however, the city blocks are
longer than in many other cities, so distances can be deceiving.
Though taxi fares are low, cabs can be hard to find on the street.
If walking and public transportation aren't your things, it's best
to rent a car or plan to call for taxis.

Salt Lake has a very workable public transportation system. A
Free Fare Zone for travel by bus covers a 15-square-block area
downtown and on Capitol Hill. A light rail system, called TRAX,
moves passengers quickly around the city and to the suburbs
south of Salt Lake. The north–south light-rail route begins at the
Delta Center and ends at 9800 South; there are 16 stations along
the way, and 11 have free park-and-ride lots. The east–west
route begins at the University of Utah and ends at Main Street.
For $2 you can buy an all-day ticket good for unlimited rides on
both buses and TRAX.

Round-trip bus service to the ski resorts (Solitude, Brighton,
Snowbird, or Alta) costs $1.75 each way; most other bus routes
cost $1 per ride. In addition, several taxi and shuttle companies
provide transportation between Salt Lake City and the ski
resorts for about $55 round-trip. A free, efficient, Park City
shuttle bus serves all the area resorts and hotels. Taxi service
within Provo and Ogden is best accessed by phone, as these
cities don't have the population to warrant a large number of
cabs.

➤ **INFORMATION: Canyon Transportation** (tel. 801/255–1841 or
800/255–1841). **Lewis Bros. Stages** (tel. 801/359–8677 or 800/826–

5844). **Park City Transportation** (tel. 435/649–8567 or 800/637–3803). **Express Shuttle** (tel. 801/596–1600 or 800/397–0773). **UTA** (tel. 801/743–3882 or 888/743–3882, www.rideuta.com).

Travel Agencies

A good travel agent puts your needs first. Look for an agency that has been in business at least five years, emphasizes customer service, and has someone on staff who specializes in your destination. In addition, **make sure the agency belongs to a professional trade organization.** The American Society of Travel Agents (ASTA)—the largest and most influential in the field with more than 26,000 members in some 170 countries—maintains and enforces a strict code of ethics and will step in to help mediate any agent-client disputes if necessary. ASTA (whose motto is "Without a travel agent, you're on your own") also maintains a Web site that includes a directory of agents. (If a travel agency is also acting as your tour operator, *see* Buyer Beware in Tours & Packages, *above*.)

➤ **LOCAL AGENT REFERRALS: American Society of Travel Agents** (ASTA; 1101 King St., Suite 200, Alexandria, VA 22314, tel. 800/965–2782 24-hr hot line, fax 703/739–7642, www.astanet.com). **Association of British Travel Agents** (68–71 Newman St., London W1T 3AH, U.K., tel. 020/7637–2444, fax 020/7637–0713, www.abtanet.com). **Association of Canadian Travel Agents** (130 Albert St., Suite 1705, Ottawa, Ontario K1P 5G4, Canada, tel. 613/237–3657, fax 613/237–7052, www.acta.net). **Australian Federation of Travel Agents** (Level 3, 309 Pitt St., Sydney NSW 2000, Australia, tel. 02/9264–3299, fax 02/9264–1085, www.afta.com.au). **Travel Agents' Association of New Zealand** (Level 5, Paxus House, 79 Boulcott St., Box 1888, Wellington 10033, New Zealand, tel. 04/499–0104, fax 04/499–0827, www.taanz.org.nz).

Visitor Information

The Salt Lake Convention and Visitors Bureau is open weekdays 8:30–5 and weekends 9–5.

▶ **TOURIST INFORMATION: Bridgerland** (160 N. Main St., Logan 84321, tel. 435/752–2161 or 800/882–4433). **Brigham City Chamber of Commerce** (6 N. Main St., Brigham City 84302, tel. 435/723–3931). **Golden Spike Empire** (2501 Wall Ave., Ogden 84401, tel. 801/627–8288 or 800/255–8824, www.ogdencvb.org). **Great Salt Lake Country** (90 S. West Temple St., Salt Lake City 84101, tel. 801/521–2822). **Heber Valley County Chamber of Commerce** (475 N. Main St., Heber 84032, tel. 435/654–3666, www.hebervalleycc.org). **Park City Chamber of Commerce/Convention and Visitors Bureau** (Box 1630, Park City 84060, tel. 435/649–6100 or 800/453–1360, www.parkcityinfo.com). **Salt Lake Convention and Visitors Bureau** (90 S. West Temple St., Salt Lake City 84101, tel. 801/521–2822, www.saltlake.org). **Ski Utah** (150 W. 500 South St., Salt Lake City 84101, tel. 801/534–1779, www.skiutah.com). **Springville Chamber of Commerce** (50 S. Main St., Springville 84663, tel. 801/489–4681). **Utah County Convention and Visitors Bureau** (51 S. University Ave., Suite 111, Provo 84601, tel. 801/370–8393 or 800/222–8824, www.utahvalley.org/cvb). **Utah Travel Council** (Council Hall, Capitol Hill, 300 N. State St., Salt Lake City, 84114, tel. 801/538–1030; 800/200–1160 for brochures; 801/521–8102 for ski reports, fax 801/538–1399).

Web Sites

Do check out the World Wide Web when planning your trip. You'll find everything from weather forecasts to virtual tours of famous cities. Be sure to visit Fodors.com (www.fodors.com), a complete travel-planning site. You can research prices and book plane tickets, hotel rooms, rental cars, vacation packages, and more. In addition, you can post your pressing questions in the Travel Talk section and, in the site's Rants & Raves section, read comments about some of the restaurants and hotels in this book—and chime in yourself. Other planning tools include a currency converter and weather reports, and there are loads of links to travel resources.

The Utah site, www.utah.com is rather cut-and-dried, but it does give plenty of listings. Also keep in mind that just about every town, park, and attraction has its own Web site, often jam-packed with pertinent information. Park sites are particularly helpful to read for safety precautions.

When to Go

Hotels in major tourist destinations book up early, especially in July and August, and hikers crowd the backcountry from June through Labor Day. Ski resorts buzz from December to early April, especially during Christmas and Presidents Day holiday weeks. If you don't mind sometimes capricious weather, spring and fall are opportune seasons to visit. Rates drop and crowds are nonexistent. Spring is a good time for fishing, rafting on rivers swollen with snowmelt, birding, and wildlife-viewing. In fall trees splash the mountainsides with golds and reds, the fish are spawning, and the angling is excellent.

CLIMATE

Summer begins in late June or early July. Fall begins in September, often with a week of unsettled weather around mid-month, followed by four to six gorgeous weeks of Indian summer—frosty nights and warm days. Winter creeps in during November, and deep snows have arrived by December. Temperatures usually hover near freezing by day, thanks to the surprisingly warm mountain sun, dropping considerably overnight. Winter tapers off in March, though snow lingers into April on valley bottoms and into July on mountain passes.

➤ **FORECASTS: Weather Channel Connection** (tel. 900/932–8437), 95¢ per minute from a Touch-Tone phone.

What follows are the average daily maximum and minimum temperatures for Salt Lake.

SALT LAKE CITY

Jan.	35F	2C	**May**	73F	23C	**Sept.**	78F	26C
	17	- 8		44	7		48	9
Feb.	41F	5C	**June**	82F	28C	**Oct.**	66F	19C
	24	- 4		51	11		39	4
Mar.	51F	11C	**July**	91F	33C	**Nov.**	48F	9C
	30	- 1		60	16		28	- 2
Apr.	62F	17C	**Aug.**	89F	32C	**Dec.**	39F	4C
	37	3		60	16		21	- 6

INDEX

FODOR'S POCKET SALT LAKE CITY AND THE WASATCH RANGE

EDITOR: Laura M. Kidder

Editorial Contributors: Kate Boyes, Christina Knight, Gayen Wharton, Tom Wharton

Editorial Production: Linda K. Schmidt

Maps: David Lindroth, *cartographer*; Bob Blake and Rebecca Baer, *map editors*

Design: Fabrizio La Rocca, *creative director*; Tigist Getachew, *art director*

Production/Manufacturing: Robert B. Shields

Cover Photograph: Richard D. McClain/Mira

COPYRIGHT

First Edition

ISBN 0–676–90490–4

IMPORTANT TIP

Although all prices, opening times, and other details in this book are based on information supplied to us at press time, changes occur all the time in the travel world, and Fodor's cannot accept responsibility for facts that become outdated or for inadvertent errors or omissions. So **always confirm information when it matters**, especially if you're making a detour to visit a specific place.

SPECIAL SALES

Fodor's Travel Publications are available at special discounts for bulk purchases for sales promotions or premiums. Special editions, including personalized covers, excerpts of existing guides, and corporate imprints, can be created in large quantities for special needs. For more information, contact your local bookseller or write to Special Markets, Fodor's Travel Publications, 280 Park Avenue, New York, NY 10017. Inquiries from Canada should be directed to your local Canadian bookseller or sent to Random House of Canada, Ltd., Marketing Department, 2775 Matheson Boulevard East, Mississauga, Ontario L4W 4P7. Inquiries from the United Kingdom should be sent to Fodor's Travel Publications, 20 Vauxhall Bridge Road, London SW1V 2SA, England.

PRINTED IN THE UNITED STATES OF AMERICA

10 9 8 7 6 5 4 3 2 1